Why Good Clients
Fire
Great Companies

© 2012, Tenacity® Inc. Third Edition
ISBN:0-9665438-3-2

Published by Tenacity Inc., Roswell, Georgia
www.tenacity.com
Cover design by Joe Voisin
Cover photo by Carie Minton
eBook Creation by
NightGlass Media Group

Why Good Clients
Fire
Great Companies

Contents

(From John) For Boots and Alice. I miss you both so much.

(From Steve) To my great wife Bonnie, my great son Dan and his great wife Jess, your encouragement and inspiration means the world to me. I couldn't love you more.

Acknowledgments

There are so many people to thank, but a few were absolutely central to the writing of this book.

Each of our partners deserves a "high five." Bill Edmundson, Chris McCarthy, Marty Zobel and John Douglas, thanks!

We're glad that Steve's name shares the cover in addition to John's. Steve's insights regarding Relevant Value^{sm} opened our eyes to so many possibilities in helping our clients retain their contracts. His contributions to this book and to our company are simply invaluable.

Kate Ravin did an outstanding job editing the book. The extent to which the book is readable is a tribute to Kate's editing, not our writing. Kate, you are one in a million.

The leadership from our client firms allowed us to test, learn, and retest our theories. We can't say "thank you" enough to Michel Landel, president of Sodexo, Tony Alibrio, past president of the Health Care Division of Sodexo, Dick Macedonia, president of the

Why Good Clients
Fire
Great Companies

Health Care Division of Sodexo, Glenn Davenport, chairman of Morrison Management Specialists, Dwight Winstead, president of Owen Healthcare, Jim Reese, chief operating officer of Randstad Staffing-USA, Mike Pfeiffer, president of Correctional Medical Services, Jerry Blalock, executive vice president of ProBusiness, and Dave Fitzgerald, president of Fitzgerald & Company, an InterPublic Group company. I really owe you guys! Thanks for your faith and trust.

Dudley Abbe, Humberto Patorniti, Joan Conner, Lisa Galanti, Chip Kent and Connie Arceneaux, you guys make it all worthwhile. Thanks for making our process part of who you are and what you stand for.

And Dudley, you are now "famous" for your thoughts on the incumbent's advantage. Thanks!

Special thanks to Sandi Clark-Martin, Bill Edmundson, Dennis Good, Gary Jones, Karen Liamos, Brad Linden, Jay Marvin, Terry Mitchell, Jim Murphy, Darlene Scalese, Scott Skorik, Ed Wang, Marty White, Dave Woodrow, and Bonnie Wurzbacher for reading the final copy of the manuscript and providing their insights and recommendations.

Why Good Clients
Fire
Great Companies

Carol Alesso, Tony Ahse, Tony Alibrio, John Ames, Mike
Bendinelli, Jodi Berlin, Bob Bianchi, Kirk Bogue, Eddie
Bonds, Anita Bowers, Peri Bridger, Gerard Bridi, Ted Bryant,
George Chavel, Mark Clark, Pat Connolly, Cathy Cooney,
Scott Corbett, Keith Cullinan, Les Dass, Dick Desrochers,
Jim DeVos, Gene Dolloff, Geri Ehrlich, Daryl Evans, Mark
Fagan, Dave Freytag, Gary Gaddy, Boscoe Godfrey, Keith
Goding, Dawn Himes, Mark Johnson, Gary Jones, Shelly
Kalfas, Kurt Kruger, Larry Krouk, Jim Lafond, John
Larochelle, Scott Loretan, Bari Love, Karla Lux, Dick
Macedonia, Jay Marvin, Naomi McKenzie, Kelly McMurry,
Dick Melgard, Dick Miles, Tom Mulligan, John Neidecker,
Bill Nestel, Paul O'Conner, Chuck O'Dell, Tony O'Haire,
Jim Paddock, Pete Pedone, Sally Powers, Bob Rasmussen,
Matt Reiter, Bob Roller, Brian Sarris, Bob Schafer, Dave
Scholz, Bob Schondelmeier, Tucker Schuldt, George
Schoener, Lou Scrizzi, Patrick Scullin, Chuck Shea, Wayne
Stockbridge, Mark Toomey, Jerry Underhill, Greg Verone,
Hickley Waguespack, Tracey Watson, Todd Wiebusch, Bob
Wood, Marty Zobel, Judy Zola, and Ed Zost, thanks for all
your help, friendship and support.

Why Good Clients
Fire
Great Companies

To Fred O'Brien ..."OB," we've watched you for years now. As far as we're concerned, you're the model for every operating vice president we would ever hope to work with. Thanks for setting the standard and showing everyone that it can be done. You do everything we've ever talked about naturally. As you've told us so many times, "This ain't rocket science!" Keep "thinking clients first!"

To all the vice presidents, multi-unit managers, and account managers in each of the companies we work with, thanks. It all comes down to your walking the talk.

Why Good Clients
Fire
Great Companies

Preface

This is the second book we've written on client and contract retention. The first, *What Your Clients Won't Tell You and Your Managers Don't Know,* was published first in 1994 and again in 1997, 1999, 2001, 2006 and 2012. Currently in its seventh printing, it has sold more than 205,000 copies and been read by managers in just about every segment of the service management industry.

What Your Clients Won't Tell You and Your Managers Don't Know introduced Tenacity Incorporated's Clients for Life® client retention process and describes the important considerations in keeping the clients and contracts you've worked so hard to get. We'm gratified that our process currently helps protect over $20 billion in contracts for some of the world's largest and best service management companies.

"Why Good Clients Fire Great Companies" builds on the foundation laid in that first effort. If you've ever lost a client when every measurement tool at your disposal suggested you would renew the contract, read on. This book can help you understand why "doing a good job," saving your clients money, and/or having high client satisfaction scores simply

Why Good Clients
Fire
Great Companies

aren't enough to guarantee a renewal. Good clients *do* fire great companies. At Tenacity Incorporated, we believe we understand what can be done to keep that from happening.

We urge you to reflect on what's happening at your own accounts as you learn along with Jack, Bonnie, and A.J. Think about the insights Jack shares regarding Revelation X^{sm} and Relevant Value and ask yourself if they don't help explain some of your past clients' decisions—decisions you never anticipated and losses you'll never forget.

Most of all, we urge you to *use* what you learn.

Thanks for your interest in our work and for allowing us to share some of our more recent thoughts on keeping your clients—*for life*.

Please note:

Why Good Clients
Fire
Great Companies

Before You Begin

If you've read *"What Your Clients Won't Tell You and Your Managers Don't Know"*, turn to the first chapter and dive right in. You're already familiar with the characters and the processes in the story.

If this is your first exposure to our work, you'll benefit from reading a little bit about the people you're about to meet and some of the processes they refer to.

You might also want to look at the appendix in the back of this book. It's taken from *"What Your Clients Won't Tell You and Your Managers Don't Know"* and will provide you additional insight into Tenacity's Clients for Life process.

Jack used to be the senior vice president of operations for Service Enterprises. He's been retired for a few years and occasionally does consulting work for the company. During Jack's tenure, his operations organization had 100 percent client retention. They *never* lost a contract. Although Jack pooh-poohs his achievement, the fact is, he's a living legend in the industry.

Why Good Clients
Fire
Great Companies

As Jack neared retirement, he chose Bonnie as his successor, teaching her everything she needed to know about the Clients for Life® client-retention process he had developed. He's never regretted the decision to have Bonnie carry on his legacy.

Bonnie recently spent two years as the company's chief operations officer and kept Jack's record intact. She'd learned her lessons well. Everyone supported her promotion to the presidency of Service Enterprises eighteen months ago. The company has continued to grow under her leadership and is widely acknowledged as the employer of choice within the industry.

While Bonnie is extraordinarily capable, she sometimes calls upon her old friend and mentor for help in solving a business problem. She values Jack's judgment, trusts his insights, and knows she can speak candidly with him about anything.

A.J. is one of Bonnie's regional vice presidents and her star pupil. Although it may be a few years before he occupies the corner office in one of the company's divisions, that's where he's headed. A Southern boy schooled in the Ivy League, A.J. inspires loyalty in clients and employees alike. When he tells you something, you can take it to the bank. There just isn't a better operating person anywhere in the industry. A.J.'s only had two "bosses" in his entire career: Jack and Bonnie.

Why Good Clients
Fire
Great Companies

Clients for Life processes:

Right Clients/Right Terms®: A set of measurable criteria established by the senior management of the company that not only guides its sales force in selecting potential clients and but also details the terms under which the organization will enter into a contract.

Expectations Session℠: A meeting held annually at an existing account (usually at the client's location) just ahead of budget time. The session is attended by anyone from the client's side who can hire or fire and/or who makes influential assessments of the service management company's performance. The service management company sends its key managers who have day-to-day or oversight responsibility for the account. The meeting's objective is to define and prioritize the mutual expectations of the organizations and the individuals representing them.

Transition Meeting℠: A meeting held after the sale is made *but before a contract is signed or operations begin*, involving the clients who made the decision to employ the service management company, the sales people who sold the contract, and the operations team that will provide day-to-day stewardship of the account. The meeting's objective is to define and prioritize the mutual expectations of the organizations and the individuals representing them. It is similar to an Expectations Session but is held at a *new* account.

Transition Lite Meetingsm: A meeting held whenever a key client changes after the contract begins. This meeting helps the new decision-maker understand why the service management company was hired, what the key expectations were when the contract was signed, what the service management company has accomplished to date, which projects are currently in process, and those that are planned for the near future.

The meeting then discusses the new decision-maker's expectations and whether or not they are consistent with the expectations of the existing client-management team. If the expectations are consistent, the account management team will continue with their current projects and priorities. If the new decision-maker's expectations are *inconsistent* with what has previously been agreed to, the account manager will suggest that a new Expectations Session be held.

Why Good Clients *Fire* Great Companies

Web of Influence®: Predicated on the notion that no company should ever allow its success to become dependent on any one individual, a Web of Influence is created when each person representing the service management company establishes business relationships with at least three other people in the client's organization. Ideally, these relationships should be with their direct counterpart, a person that reports to their direct counterpart, and the person their direct counterpart reports to. These relationships should be created both vertically and horizontally within the client's organization.

Expectations Paradox℠: Based on expectations management theory, the Expectations Paradox proves that the more you do for a client, the more clients expect of you. You can set the bar so high that even *you* can't consistently jump over it. Therefore, each service provided to clients should be accompanied by communication that helps them understand whether or not that level of service can be sustained.

FreshEyes Review®: An independent, third-party assessment of the service management company's performance. Ideally, interviews are conducted with each client in the Web of Influence. The discussions center on three things: whether or not the firm is meeting the client's expectations; the quality of the relationships between the individuals representing both organizations; and whether or not the service provider has solved the problems they were hired to solve and are bringing innovation to the client's organization.

Why Good Clients
Fire
Great Companies

The Call

Why Good Clients
Fire
Great Companies

Bonnie sat at her desk, staring out the window for what seemed like hours. She stared right through the beauty of the landscaped view from her fourth-floor office at Service Enterprises. Her thoughts raced from the cancellation notice in her hand, to A.J.'s resignation on her desk, to the feelings of embarrassment and failure in her gut. She just couldn't believe the news she'd received that morning.

After all, it was only last quarter that the results from Service Enterprises' annual client satisfaction telephone survey had been published. Gambra Incorporated had given Service Enterprises rave reviews—high marks in every category.

Her files were filled with correspondence from Gambra's representatives praising A.J.'s leadership as regional vice president and the skills of his entire account team. She'd been to Gambra herself less than six months ago to review Service Enterprises' performance and to fulfill her obligations under the Web of Influence℠ that A.J. and his managers had established. She would have bet anything that the relationships were solid and that Service Enterprises' technical performance was sound.

But no matter how much Bonnie wanted it not to be true, the fact remained: Gambra Incorporated, the largest account in her company, had just refused to renew its contract.

Why Good Clients
Fire
Great Companies

A.J. had received the cancellation notice that morning and, after calling Bonnie, had forwarded it to her so she could read it for herself. Consistent with the policy Bonnie had established years ago in her operations organization, the resignations of A.J. and his account managers accompanied the cancellation letter.

Her mind wandered back to the day she implemented the policy and to the hue and cry that followed. To quell the HR concerns over "losing good people," she made two things clear to her organization. First, she shared her belief that *personal accountability* was the lynchpin of the Clients for Life process and that everyone would be expected to fulfill their individual responsibilities - no exceptions. And, perhaps as important, she made it clear that as long as the Clients for Life process had been followed by her managers, she would *never* accept a resignation stemming from a lost client.

Still, Bonnie didn't anticipate the emotions she felt in seeing the resignation letters, especially A.J.'s. He was one of her best. He was also one of the best regional vice presidents in the industry, on a fast track for more responsibility and widely regarded as a leading candidate for a division presidency of one of Service Enterprises' new start-ups. Bonnie took pride not only in A.J.'s achievement but also in having been his mentor since Jack had introduced them years earlier. But now, A.J.'s resignation sat on her desk. Even though she doubted she would find cause to accept it, her heart ached every time she looked at it.

Over and over the same question pounded in her head: "How can this be happening?"

Every internal measure the company used suggested that Gambra Incorporated would renew its contract. There hadn't been any significant blips in the relationship. Bonnie had imagined that she and A.J. would be celebrating a renewal, not getting ready to deal with the company's first client loss since she became president.

Bonnie's internal monologue kept her from noticing that Lindsey, her secretary, was standing in the doorway.

"Bonnie," Lindsey said softly, knowing how shaken Bonnie had been by the news.

"Yes?"

Lindsey had never heard Bonnie sound so detached and emotionally drained. "I have Jack on the line," she replied.

Why Good Clients
Fire
Great Companies

"Oh, thanks." Bonnie struggled to collect her thoughts. She wasn't quite sure what she would say to Jack, but she knew he was one of the few people who could help her make sense of this—if anyone could. And she had to be certain she'd considered every aspect of the situation before she called her client later that day.

"Hi, Bonnie!" Jack's voice was cheery as ever.

"Hi, Jack," Bonnie tried to sound natural. "Thanks for returning my call so quickly."

"No problem. My tee time is'nt for another two hours. What's up? It's not like you to call me this early."

"Jack," Bonnie faltered, "I have a problem—a big one—and I need you to help me think through my response."

From Bonnie's strained and urgent tone, Jack realized her news must be significant. He'd known her for years now, and he had rarely sensed the concern now apparent in her voice.

"My time is your time, Bonnie. What's going on?"

Bonnie's voice cracked a little as she answered, "I think we've lost our first account."

Why Good Clients
Fire
Great Companies

At these words, Jack experienced the sinking feeling that accompanies the totally unexpected. He tried to mask his concern as he said, "You must be in shock. Which account?"

"It's Gambra Incorporated."

"Gambra? Are you kidding me? They're one of your biggest. What happened?"

"That's just it—I don't know! Everything we measure says they should have renewed with no problem. I'm stunned, and A.J. is ... well ... I can't even begin to describe how devastated he is."

"Are you booked later this morning?" Jack asked.

"I've got a couple of meetings but nothing that I can't reschedule. Why?"

"I'd like to stop by and talk face to face—unless you want to do this by phone?"

"Oh, Jack, I'd really appreciate it if you'd come by," Bonnie confessed, her relief palpable. "I have to call Gambra's CEO later this afternoon, and I need to think through my response to the cancellation notice. No one could help me do that better than you. And it would be good to see you, even under these circumstances."

"I can be there in an hour," Jack assured her. "In the meantime, why don't you ask Lindsey to pull together all the pertinent information on Gambra?"

"I've already asked her to get started on it," Bonnie replied. "She's given me the recap from the last Expectations Session^{sm}, the current work plan and progress reports, the notes on the Transition Lite^{sm} meetings we conducted with the CEO and CFO when they came on board, the. . ."

"Wait a minute," Jack interrupted. "When did Gambra get a new CEO and CFO?"

"About eight months ago," Bonnie said. "I met both of them about five or six months ago, when we reviewed the expectations they had shared during the Transition Lite meeting with A.J.'s account manager. I thought they were fine with the direction we had established for the account. And they seemed to appreciate everything we'd done for them."

"Well—" Jack blurted.

"Yeah, I know. Obviously, I wasn't listening very well or we wouldn't be talking about this now."

"You're a great listener, Bonnie. Maybe they didn't give you the chance to listen."

"What do you mean?"

"Let's save that until later," Jack suggested. "What other information do we have?"

"What else?" Bonnie murmured, sifting through the files on her desk. "There's last year's FreshEyes Review^{sm}, the current Web of Influence status form, and the recap of the Team Account Retention Plan^{sm}."

"When did the account group update the T.A.R.P. ^{sm} form?"

"Let me see. . . It looks like it was done a little under a year ago."

"Sounds like you've got a good start. See if you can find

anything else that sheds light on the situation, and I'll be there soon."

"Thanks, Jack," Bonnie said fervently, adding, "By the way, I'd like A.J. to join us."

"Couldn't agree more."

"Good. He's out of the office, but I'll leave a voicemail for him. I know he'll want to be part of this."

"I'm on my way, Bon. Try to relax and keep perspective, okay?"

As Jack hung up the phone, he imagined Bonnie sitting at her desk, staring vacantly out the window. He knew how she must be feeling, and when he realized that because of company protocol, she could very well lose her best VP as well as her biggest account, his heart sank in sympathy.

In retirement, he'd watched Bonnie rise to the presidency of the firm. He cherished the mentoring he'd provided early in her career and admired her passion for the Clients for Life® client-retention process he'd shared with her. Using its principles, Bonnie had been able to generate significantly higher margins in each of the divisions she managed on her way to the top. She'd realized, as he had, that keeping existing clients is much more profitable than the client churning typical in most service management organizations.

Even though Jack's IRA profited handsomely from the increases in Service Enterprises' stock price, his love for the company and its people was what kept him active and willing to provide his consulting expertise whenever they called.

As he grabbed his car keys, Jack could easily relate to Bonnie's alternating feelings of bewilderment, anger, and helplessness. He'd received similar news more than twenty years ago, but the incident remained as vivid in his memory as if it had happened yesterday. "You never forget what it feels like to lose your first key account," he said to himself.

Why Good Clients
Fire
Great Companies

Why?

Why Good Clients
Fire
Great Companies

Jack blinked in surprise as the Service Enterprises office complex swung into view. He felt as if he'd just pulled out of his own driveway. Totally absorbed in thoughts of his conversation with Bonnie and the meeting about to take place, he didn't remember one minute of the thirty-five mile trip.

Pulling into one of the visitor's parking spaces reminded Jack that his days as Service Enterprises' VP of operations were long gone. As a consultant, he realized that he wouldn't be able to *fix* anything. That would be up to Bonnie and A.J. But he could help them analyze what had happened, think through their options, and select the best course of action. And he believed this kind of support was all Bonnie expected from him.

As Jack locked the car door, he glanced up at Bonnie's office window. He knew she was strong and talented enough to deal with this adversity. But he also knew that the lessons of the next twenty-four hours would stay with her for the rest of her career.

"Lindsey, you look younger every time I see you," Jack exclaimed as he crossed the office threshold.

Why Good Clients
Fire
Great Companies

"That's because I'm half your age and your vision isn't what it used to be!" Lindsey parried.

They both laughed, exchanging smiles and a quick hug.

"Bonnie's down the hall with Tracey, our controller," Lindsey reported. "I'll let her know you're here, but she said she might be a few minutes. Can I get you some coffee or a Coke?"

"Coffee, black," Jack replied. "Hold the sugar. I'm putting on a few pounds, and I'm sweet enough already."

"You're right—on both counts!" Lindsey returned. Looking more serious, she added, "Bonnie's left you a pile of Gambra files."

Jack moved quickly to Bonnie's desk, sorted through the stack, and selected the file marked "Gambra Incorporated-Web." As he reviewed the information on Service Enterprises' Web of Influence at Gambra Incorporated, Jack noticed what appeared to be a significant number of changes in the client's personnel over the past year. Service Enterprises' primary liaison at Gambra Incorporated had changed twice in that time. And, as Bonnie had mentioned, the changes also included a new CEO and CFO, who had arrived within six weeks of each other, eight months ago.

As Jack reviewed these entries, the warning, *"When people change, everything has the potential to change,"* so crucial to his mentoring of Bonnie years ago, raced through his head. Jack took out his yellow legal pad, noted the changes in personnel, and picked up the file marked "Gambra Incorporated-Expectations/Transition Lite meetings."

This file was designed to track several factors: the expectations of Gambra's management team; the changes in those expectations during the course of Gambra's relationship with Service Enterprises; any reactions relevant to those expectations on the part of new managers at Gambra; and the plans designed to fulfill client expectations at each stage of the relationship between Service Enterprises and Gambra Incorporated.

Jack knew that each year, typically at budget time, A.J.'s managers would meet with the Gambra Incorporated management team to review how well Service Enterprises' performance had met the client's expectations and to establish new expectations for the coming year. A.J.'s account manager, Karen, would then create a plan to deliver on the expectations identified during this meeting. Each month, as she made progress against the targets they mutually established, Karen would review the successes they had enjoyed and document them in this file.

Jack also knew that whenever a change occurred in the client's management team, Karen would schedule a meeting with the new manager within thirty days of his or her arrival. This was called the Transition Lite meeting, and its objectives were twofold: educating the new decision-maker as to Gambra's current expectations, and reviewing the value Service Enterprises had provided.

Transition Lite meetings were well choreographed. As account manager for Service Enterprises, Karen would review the client's history, carefully detailing the key problems Service Enterprises had inherited as well as the solutions it had provided. Next, the conversation would focus on Gambra's existing expectations and the status of key projects currently under way. Finally, Karen would offer the new decision-maker a look at future projects and describe how they were intended to meet the expectations previously established by his or her organization.

Karen would then ask the new decision-maker a series of questions designed to elicit his or her expectations of Service Enterprises. For Karen, listening to these responses was critical. If the new person's expectations were similar to those of the existing management team, there was no need to worry; the plans to meet them probably were already in place. However, if the new decision-maker's expectations differed fundamentally from those of other client managers, the new expectations had to be dealt with and incorporated into the operating plan.

Karen's response was determined by the position of the new decision-maker. If he or she was a senior manager such as a CEO, COO or CFO, Karen knew it was time to call for a new Expectations Session with the client's entire management team. Otherwise, she'd be caught between a rock and a hard place. There was no way to succeed if she continued to work on expectations the client management team considered important but the new senior manager didn't agree with.

By the same token, if Karen simply began to work on what was important to the new senior manager, the existing client management team members would wonder why she wasn't following through on the commitments made during *their* Expectations Session. A new session, in which the client's entire management team could listen to the new senior manager's expectations and adjust their own accordingly, was the only sensible course of action.

Jack was consistently amazed that other firms—even their direct competitors—hadn't figured out that the decisive thing is not *what you do* but instead, *what you do relative to the client's expectations.* All the competitors seemed to do was sell *their* ideas and try to convince the new decision-maker to take action on *their* agendas.

As Jack browsed through the Gambra Incorporated file, he noticed something that frightened him: there didn't appear to have been a Transition Lite meeting with the new CEO. At least, there wasn't a record of one in the file.

The notes also told Jack something else. While the new CFO's expectations were not surprising, they were significant. She was looking for a 20 percent reduction in overall costs. What *was* surprising, however, was that the file didn't contain any notes on Service Enterprise's response to the CFO's requests regarding cost reduction.

"It isn't like A.J. or Bonnie to let something like this go unresolved," Jack thought to himself, making additional notes on his legal pad. He quickly flipped through the files and picked up the one marked "Gambra Incorporated-P&L."

Jack still admired the diligence with which Service Enterprises kept comprehensive records of its stewardship of client accounts. He knew that everything he needed to understand the company's financial transactions would be in this file. And his background in operations told him just what to look for.

"Man, this is great performance," Jack said aloud as he opened the file and found the key indicators he sought.

A quick review of the numbers made two things clear to him. First, Service Enterprises was doing an excellent job of controlling costs at Gambra Incorporated. Since Service Enterprises had assumed responsibility for the account, operating costs were down over 40 percent, despite annual increases in the cost of supplies, labor, and benefits.

Second, the fees Service Enterprises charged Gambra Incorporated had continued to increase because of the type of contract in place. But that was good news. Essentially, it was a "pay-for-performance" contract. And since Service Enterprises had been reducing costs, and its fees were tied to cost reduction while keeping customer satisfaction high, the fees had gone up year after year.

It was a heck of a deal for Gambra Incorporated—they'd saved millions.

Just as Jack leaned forward to pick up the folder marked "Gambra Incorporated-Team Account Retention Plan (T.A.R.P)." Lindsey arrived with his coffee.

"Here ya go," Lindsey said, handing him the cup.

"Thanks, Lindsey."

"Bonnie asked me to tell you she'll be here in about five minutes, but A.J. can't make it until around noon. He has a client commitment," Lindsey said.

"No problem," Jack replied. "Thanks again for the coffee."

"Any time, Jack. Let me know if there's anything else you need," Lindsey called over her shoulder as she headed for her desk in the anteroom.

"One thing," Jack interjected. "Are these all the files on Gambra?"

Why Good Clients *Fire* Great Companies

"All that we have. A.J. might have a couple with him. Would you like me to leave him a voicemail and ask him to bring whatever he has this afternoon?"

"Please."

As Lindsey shut the door to Bonnie's office, Jack sat back, took a sip of coffee and reflected on what he'd seen in the files so far: new decision-makers in key positions, frequent changes in the contact administrator position, new—and apparently unresolved—expectations from key clients, a breech in company protocol in that the Transition Lite meeting with the CEO might not have taken place, and fees that continued to grow despite the CFO's concern about overall costs.

"I know A.J. and Bonnie must see the same things," Jack thought to himself. "I'm not going to rush to judgment until we've talked this through."

With that, he picked up the "Gambra Incorporated-T.A.R.P." folder and started to read.

Why Good Clients
      Fire
Great Companies

T.A.R.P.:
The "Go To" Folder

Why Good Clients *Fire* Great Companies

If there was one document that Jack always went to in a crisis, it was the T.A.R.P. form. He'd learned from experience that the Team Account Retention Plan typically held the key to the problems confronting him. As he began to review the T.A.R.P. information in the Gambra Incorporated file, Jack's mind wandered back to the time when he'd conceived the T.A.R.P. process.

The T.A.R.P. process evolved from a revelation that had occurred to Jack after more than a decade in the business: there is a fundamental difference between *client satisfaction* and *client retention*. Moreover, these two outcomes had to be managed with entirely separate processes.

T.A.R.P. was born when Jack came to think of satisfaction and retention as related (like cousins) rather than equivalent (like identical twins). While he agreed that he'd be crazy not to want high levels of client satisfaction at his sites, his thinking really progressed once he accepted that high client satisfaction alone was not enough. Achieving 100 percent client retention required new thinking, skills, and processes.

At the time, Service Enterprises' business had been changing slowly but significantly. During its early years, the company had offered one service and dealt with one client location,

Why Good Clients
Fire
Great Companies

using a simple "fee-for-service" contract. Essentially, one on-site manager was responsible for everything that had anything to do with each account.

However, as Service Enterprises grew, it began to expand the number of services offered. Instead of employing a single on-site manager, Service Enterprises often had a general manager supervise several technical specialists responsible for various aspects of each account.

Service Enterprises' clients and contracts had become more complicated, as well. Instead of dealing with one location, Service Enterprises was beginning to serve multiple client sites, which might be located hundreds, if not thousands, of miles apart. And contracts had progressed from simple fee schedules to "performance-based," "risk-sharing," "benchmarked," contracts that often couldn't be interpreted consistently by the very people who had negotiated them.

The nature of the client interaction had changed, too. Instead of dealing with a single client decision-maker, Service Enterprises managers often dealt with a decision-making unit composed of local, regional, and sometimes national contacts within the client organization.

Why Good Clients *Fire* Great Companies

It was no secret that Service Enterprises' work was becoming not only more complicated but much different from what the company had dealt with historically. And it was obvious that no single account manager could ever keep track of—or influence—all the people affecting the viability of a contract and the longevity of a client relationship.

In response to these conditions and his realization of the difference between client satisfaction and client retention, Jack and his team invented the Team Account Retention Plan. It was based on a very simple notion: bring everyone who had anything to do with selling or running the account—ideally all members of the Web of Influence on Service Enterprises' side—into the same room at least once a year to discuss issues relevant to managing the business and retaining the account.

At first, these discussions weren't tightly structured; and there was lot of good give and take among participants. Over time, however, the Service Enterprises team developed a series of key questions regarding the needs of the account (and/or the client) and their own performance in meeting them. These questions became the basis for the T.A.R.P. form.

Why Good Clients *Fire* Great Companies

Two of Jack's favorite questions were, "Is the reason we were hired still valid?" and "If the reason we were hired is no longer valid, why should the client continue to retain us?" He noticed from the Gambra Incorporated document that these were the first two questions the Service Enterprises team had had to answer.

The rest of the T.A.R.P. discussions usually centered on key client expectations, problems to be solved, resource requirements, investment in equipment and personnel, competitive pressures, key performance indicators, and the status of the Web of Influence at the account. Depending on the account's size and complexity, the T.A.R.P meetings usually lasted a day or so.

From its inception, the T.A.R.P process had paid huge dividends. The perspectives shared during these meetings resulted in unique and invaluable insights among the team members—and in strategies and tactics that no single team member could have devised alone. Jack often thought the T.A.R.P sessions had enabled him to appreciate the word "synergy."

"Look at this," Jack said to himself as he reviewed the

Gambra information. "There hasn't been any significant investment in the majority of Gambra's operations in over two years. And although we've delivered significant reductions in costs since becoming responsible for their more recent acquisitions, we seem to have bottomed out in the vast majority of operations we're responsible for. Benchmarked costs at continuing operations have been reduced less than half of 1 percent in the past year. That's not going to cut it."

Jack became uneasy as he examined the file's details. In every area except the recent acquisitions, he saw an account that was coasting and living on past performance. It scared the hell out of him.

"Hey, stranger," came out of nowhere, as Bonnie burst into the room. "Long time, no see!"

"Too long," Jack replied, giving Bonnie a big hug. "But we have to stop meeting like this."

"That's the truth," she agreed. "I see you've been keeping yourself busy while I was with Tracey." Bonnie motioned toward the open folders and the notes on Jack's legal pad.

"Just trying to bring myself up to speed."

Why Good Clients
Fire
Great Companies

"Anything hit you?"

"A couple of things, but I just started looking at the T.A.R.P. form," Jack hedged.

"That always was your 'go to' form, wasn't it?"

"Still is," Jack said with a smile. "But we can go over it together a little later."

"Did Lindsey tell you that A.J. can't be here until afternoon?"

"She did, and in a way, I'm glad. It will give us an hour or so alone to talk things over."

"Where do we start?"

"Why don't you tell me how you felt about the account before you got the call from A.J.?" Jack suggested. "Obviously you were surprised by what happened."

"Jack," Bonnie said, her voice betraying her distress, "'Surprised' doesn't begin to describe how I felt. Just look at the account history." She reached for one of the files on the

Why Good Clients
Fire
Great Companies

desk. "They've had years of consistent performance under our stewardship. Costs are down more than 40 percent. We have a stable work force in place. Customer satisfaction at each of the Gambra sites is at near-record levels. We've maintained solid relationships through at least two management changes at key Gambra facilities."

Bonnie took a breath and then continued. "They didn't have one major issue at the contract renewal three years ago. And look—look at this! They rated us as high as they've ever rated us on the client satisfaction survey our corporate office conducted just six months ago."

"So you thought things were going pretty well?"

"Wouldn't you?"

"Perhaps," Jack said quietly.

"Perhaps? Come on, Jack! Why would you think anything but?"

"Before I answer that, can I ask you a question?"

"Sure."

Why Good Clients
Fire
Great Companies

"How many accounts do you have in the division now?"

"Accounts or points of service?"

"Both," Jack said, remembering there was a major distinction between the two.

"Well. . ." Bonnie paused to pull the numbers from memory, then rattled them off as they popped into her head. "We have 231 clients with 364 operations sites using one or more of the three services currently in our portfolio. The division's now doing just under $800 million on the top line," she added, anticipating Jack's next question.

"And you have four regional VPs and sixteen district managers, right?"

"Almost. We have thirteen district managers now. Everyone in the corporation got hit with the overhead reductions last year."

"Hmmm. . ." Jack did a little mental math. "And the account load is split pretty evenly between the regions and districts?"

"By and large. A few districts carry a heavier load, but I'd say you were pretty much on target."

"So, if my math is correct, each RVP is responsible for approximately sixty clients and ninety sites?"

"About," Bonnie affirmed.

"And each district manager is responsible for just under twenty clients and almost thirty operating sites?"

"That's about right. But things have changed since you were with the division. We have a lot of support people behind the DMs. They can cover a lot more accounts than they could when you were here," Bonnie explained.

"I agree with you, Bonnie, they probably can cover more accounts," Jack replied. "But how many more is something we'll want to talk about sometime."

Not wanting to get drawn into a debate on staffing ratios, he added quickly, "Just one more thing before I share my initial observations."

"Shoot."

Why Good Clients
Fire
Great Companies

"How often do *you* get to see each of your accounts each year?" Jack looked directly into Bonnie's eyes.

"Oh, that depends on what's going on. You know that, Jack," Bonnie said preemptively. "Some accounts I see on a quarterly basis. Some once a year. And you know I'd be lying if I said I get to all of them."

Bonnie had confirmed Jack's expectations. "And the last time you were at Gambra was six months ago, right?" he asked.

"Right," Bonnie agreed. "Just before the corporate research department did the client satisfaction survey."

"I thought so," Jack said with a wry smile and a quick nod of his head.

Bonnie had come to know that smile. "Spill it, Jack," she laughed. "Tell me what's going on in that bald head of yours."

"Let's grab another cup of coffee first," Jack replied.

With that, they got up and headed for the Starbucks kiosk located on the main floor of the office building.

When People Change...

Why Good Clients
Fire
Great Companies

Bonnie was glad that Jack had suggested they enjoy their
French Roast outside. The tables in the courtyard weren't
crowded at this time of the day, and they'd be able to talk
without being interrupted. Besides, after the chill of the
morning's announcement, she wanted to feel the sun's
warmth on her face.

"Okay, Jack," Bonnie said as they settled in at a table
overlooking a small waterfall, "tell me what you're
thinking."

"Before I share my impressions, would you mind if I asked
you a couple of questions?"

Bonnie couldn't help smiling to herself. "Typical Jack," she
thought. For as long as she'd known him, he'd shared what
was on his mind by asking questions and letting her come to
her own conclusions.

"Not at all," she said.

Jack put his legal pad on the table, opened it to a blank sheet,
and started scribbling. "I'm assuming Gambra had quite a
few problems years ago, when you began this contract,
right?"

"Right," Bonnie affirmed. "Clients always have a lot of problems when they hire us. I imagine that's *why* they hire us. They've usually tried to solve the problems themselves, but eventually they realize they need specialists for the issues confronting specific departments. In Gambra's case, as the company expanded through acquisitions, they brought us into their new locations to help them get things under control."

Jack nodded as he drew some lines on the legal pad. "And over the course of the contract, our company solves those problems, right?"

"Right!" Bonnie said again, realizing that mentally, Jack still hadn't left the firm. "If we didn't, we'd be out of business."

"And where are Service Enterprises' fees at the beginning of the contract?" Jack asked, adding to the diagram on the legal pad. "I mean, are they as high as you'd like them to be?"

"You know they're not. Given the competitive environment and the pressure it puts on us in many bid situations, you know we don't make what we'd like to at the beginning of the contract." We also have substantial start up costs to absorb."

"But the profitability changes with time, doesn't it?" Jack knew from experience that Bonnie had to agree.

Why Good Clients
Fire
Great Companies

"If we've taken the right clients under the right terms, and done our job well it does," she replied. "The contract gives us the opportunity to improve our profitability as we solve the client's problems and demonstrate the value of our involvement. Hopefully, we continue to become more and more efficient in driving costs down, or at least controlling them."

"Then, over time, the relationship between you and your client would look like this," Jack proposed, revealing the results of his efforts on the legal pad.

As Bonnie looked at the drawing, she recalled that Jack had an ability to express his thought processes in illustrations that were easy to understand.

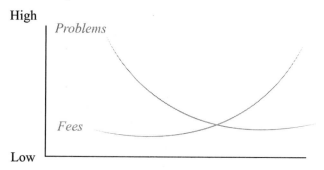

"I guess," Bonnie responded. "If I'm looking at this correctly, it shows that the client's problems are solved, and we make a fair return for our efforts over the course of the contract."

"That's an interesting way to look at it."

Jack's tone was neutral, but Bonnie could sense his disapproval. "What do you mean?" she demanded.

"Well, let's look at things from the client's perspective. But first, let me make a couple of additions to this diagram."

Jack took the legal pad, drew a few more lines and notations on it, and returned it to Bonnie.

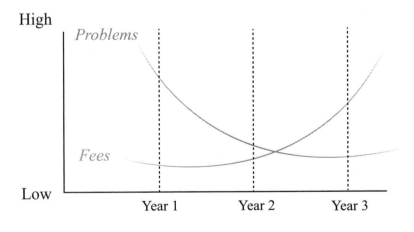

Why Good Clients
Fire
Great Companies

"Would this be a fair representation of a typical three-year contract?" he asked.

"I don't know." Bonnie was puzzled. "What are you getting at?"

"Let's take a look at what's happening in the early stages of the contract as I've shown it here," Jack said, pointing to the segment spanning the first year.

He indicated the descending line that charted client perceptions of the problems facing the organization. "Look at what's happening. The client's problems are being solved at a pretty rapid pace."

"I'll agree with that," Bonnie allowed. "That's because we've conducted a Transition Meeting^{sm} with the clients, which has given us an understanding of their problems and the priorities the client's management team places on solving them. And, as you know Jack, coming out of the Transition Meeting we also have a shared set of expectations that makes the day-to-day working relationship a lot easier. So it's possible to make significant improvements early in the contract. And that's precisely what we did with Gambra's latest acquisition."

"Exactly." Jack was pleased at how well Bonnie retained the lessons he'd taught her years ago. "And because of the competitive environment, your fees are relatively low at the beginning of the relationship." With his pencil, Jack gestured toward the ascending line that represented Service Enterprises' fees. "When you look at the situation as it's illustrated here, the client clearly is getting a huge 'bang for the buck.'"

"I see your point," Bonnie responded. "But that's just a typical start-up situation for us. We invest a lot in the early stages of the contract, knowing that we'll realize the payoff from those investments down the road. We've done just that with Gambra over the years." Privately, she wondered why Jack was belaboring the obvious.

"Not so fast," he cautioned. "Bear with me while we look at the next phase of the contract."

Sensing Bonnie's growing detachment, Jack quickly moved his pencil to the segment of the diagram marked "Year 2."

"If you've been as successful in Year 1 as you say, you begin to make a little more money in Year 2 of the contract, don't you?"

Why Good Clients
Fire
Great Companies

"Well, that depends on the contract's language," Bonnie qualified. "But for most of the deals we're involved with today, that would be true. We're paid on the basis of our performance, and if we're solving the problems in Year 1, as you've indicated in this diagram, then chances are we begin to make money somewhere in Year 2. It certainly worked that way with Gambra."

"And the primary issues the client hired you to solve are under control?"

"I guess. Naturally, we've allocated a lot of resources to the account to get the key issues under control in Year 1. So by the time 60 percent of the contract is completed—the period that spans Year 2 in your diagram—we should have the primary problems resolved, or at least have made significant progress in dealing with them."

"Okay," Jack said. "Now, let me make sure I'm clear on one more thing. Let's look at Year 3 of the contract as I've illustrated it here. What do you see happening?"

"Well," Bonnie answered slowly, concentrating on Jack's diagram for the first time, "by then we've pretty much resolved the client's issues and we're being compensated for the huge investments we made during the contract's early stages."

"So, you make a ton of money in Year 3?"

"Well, sure! But if you're saying we're making too much money for what we're doing then, you have to admit that we didn't make near what we were worth in Year 1."

"Wouldn't argue with you on that point."

"Well, then what *is* the point?" Bonnie asked in exasperation.

"Just this: the way most of your contracts—including Gambra Incorporated's—are structured, the value we deliver to the client is clear in the early stages, as the diagram shows. But as you can see, the value the client receives becomes less clear in the middle years, and from the client's perspective, that value is questionable in the final years of the relationship."

"I see that's what this diagram suggests," Bonnie objected, "but our clients understand how things work. They know our 'overcompensation' in Year 3 is a matter of the contract's structure and language—plus our willingness to be paid on the basis of improvements we make to the operation."

She continued: "They also know that if everything works the way it should, they'll be paying more for our services at the end of the contract than at the beginning. In fact, they're happy to do so because it means three things: we've been successful, their problems have been solved, and it's win-win all the way around."

"That's exactly the way it should work," Jack agreed, "*if* the people who hired you are the people you're still working for in Year 3."

"Huh?" Bonnie grunted, realizing that for at least the third time in this conversation, she was at a loss.

"May I ask you a question?" Jack proposed.

Bonnie shrugged, knowing there was little she could do to stop him.

"Do the majority of contracts you sign have a cancellation clause?"

Why Good Clients *Fire* Great Companies

"You know they do." Bonnie's patience was wearing thin. "Our clients wouldn't sign a contract if they didn't have an out, and I don't blame them. They have to protect themselves from being stuck with a management services company that isn't performing."

"And how much notification do they have to give you before canceling the contract?"

"It depends, but typically it's anywhere from thirty to ninety days."

"So, if they believe it's in their best interest to sever relations with you, they can make it happen in as little as thirty days. Is that right?"

"I guess," Bonnie admitted. "But the cancellation clause would most likely be tied to lack of performance on our part, and you know we'd never allow ourselves to get caught in that situation."

"Bonnie, believe me, I understand what a great job you do and what this company stands for," Jack assured her, "but truth be told, if a client firm wanted to cancel a contract it could. Our only recourse would be to take the organization to

Why Good Clients
Fire
Great Companies

court and let the judge decide if we'd lived up to the
conditions of the contract."

"You're right," Bonnie conceded. "We probably wouldn't
take it to court. That's lose-lose, and we don't operate that
way. If a client cancelled, I guess we'd just move on—as
long as our receivable balance was current. But that hasn't
happened to us since we've been practicing the Clients for
Life client-retention process you introduced way back when."

"Not until now," Jack said softly, not wanting to cause
Bonnie any more pain.

Bonnie simply stared and said nothing as the reality of the
Gambra Incorporated cancellation once again consumed her.

From personal experience, Jack knew what she was feeling,
and he didn't wait for her to respond. He added one more line
to the diagram and turned it back toward Bonnie.

New Client Appears

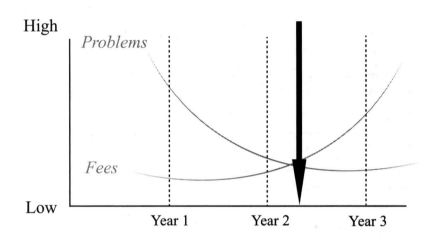

"I've added an element I think is key in helping you understand what happened," Jack said.

"New client appears," Bonnie read aloud.

"Right. Now, let me ask you a question," Jack forged ahead. "When Gambra's new CEO and CFO assumed responsibility for the operation, which way did they look—I mean, were they concerned about what happened in the past or what would happen from the point of their arrival forward?"

"I guess new executives would look at the past to some extent to learn what had happened before they got there," Bonnie reasoned. "But I imagine they're primarily concerned with what happens on their watch."

"I agree," Jack responded. "And if we use this diagram to represent the contract with Gambra, tell me what you think the new CEO and CFO saw when they assumed responsibility for the operation."

"Oh, *no!*" Bonnie gasped. "They must have seen very few problems in the areas we're responsible for and us making a ton of money while Gambra is struggling to become profitable again because of issues in other parts of its operation."

"And what must the CEO and CFO have thought about that?" Jack persisted.

"Jack, I don't know what they thought, but we *earned* that money! We worked hard to get those new acquisitions in order. Those problems didn't disappear by themselves. We invested in people and equipment, and we brought in our proprietary systems—all on their behalf. You can't look at the fact that we're making a lot of money now and forget that we operated in the red for a good bit of that contract."

"Why not?"

"Because it's not fair!" Bonnie nearly shouted, her frustration turning to anger. "No, Jack, more than that," she rushed on, "it's the way *they* wanted the contract to be. And we accepted the terms because we knew we could turn those operations around."

"So, you agreed to lose money for the first eighteen months?"

"No, we didn't! We agreed to accept the assignment based on the terms of the agreement. And we've lived up to every commitment we've made to them."

"And now you expect them to allow Service Enterprises to make 'a ton of money'—even though Gambra Incorporated is struggling to break even as a business entity?"

"Jack, I feel for Gambra, I really do. But I'm not responsible for their loss of market share in parts of the company we have nothing to do with. If they've made errors in judgment or strategic mistakes, it's their problem, not ours. The departments we run for Gambra are well managed and efficient. I won't accept the blame for their management's mistakes."

"And it seems like the new CEO and CFO aren't about to either," Jack said evenly. "They're correcting one of those 'mistakes' now—by firing Service Enterprises."

Bonnie struggled to retort, but Jack plunged ahead. "This isn't about Service Enterprises' performance. You have every right to be proud of what your team has accomplished and the way they lived up to their commitments, and I know Gambra's problems wouldn't have been solved without your interventions and expertise. But this is about a new management team inheriting a struggling operation and finding that they can take a significant amount of money to their bottom line by firing a management services company used in certain departments of the company. Basically, they feel confident they can run the problem-free operation you've put in place."

Before Bonnie could respond, Jack added, "While I can't be certain, I imagine their point of view is simple. Service

Enterprises signed a three-year contract with a thirty-day cancellation clause. Gambra paid Service Enterprises every month according to the terms of that agreement. If Service Enterprises didn't make much or even any money for the first eighteen months of the contract, that is not, and should not be, of any concern to Gambra's management."

"But—" Bonnie's impulse to defend her record was natural and strong. Still, Jack knew he had to help her get past the notion that Gambra's action was "not fair."

"The new CEO and CFO are concerned about one thing," he continued, "turning their business around and making it profitable, just as you would be if you were in their shoes. They're doing what they believe is the best thing for their business."

"Damn it, Jack!" Bonnie had given up any pretense at composure. "It's *not* the best thing for their business. Do you know what will happen to those departments if we pull our managers and systems? Inside of twelve months their costs will skyrocket. If they think they have problems in other parts of their operation now, they haven't seen anything compared to the red ink that will flow if they pull our people and systems, they'll—"

Why Good Clients
Fire
Great Companies

"Bonnie," Jack said in a tone that was firm but kind, "we both know what will happen, and while that's something we need to keep in mind as we prepare for your call to the CEO, I don't think it's the issue that led to the cancellation notice. The point is, Gambra's new management isn't looking twelve months into the future. Their focus is on effecting a turn-around *today*.

"But," Jack added with a seriousness Bonnie had rarely seen in him, "unless I'm wrong, you've got bigger problems than Gambra's cancellation. You see, unless you do something about it, I think what happened at Gambra Incorporated could happen at other contracts you manage."

Bonnie's heart plunged as she fought to respond, but she couldn't say a word.

The Value Gap

Why Good Clients
Fire
Great Companies

Bonnie was still staring at Jack's illustration when he returned with his second cup of coffee.

"Jack," she said as he sat down beside her, "I can see why you think Gambra's new CEO canceled the contract, but what on Earth makes you say other contracts are at risk?"

"That may have been an exaggeration because a lot of it depends on deal structure; but in the contracts you operate under conditions similar to the ones at Gambra Incorporated, the answer is really very simple," Jack said with assurance.

"And that is?"

"You're very good at what you do."

"Huh?" Again Bonnie wished she could come up with a more intelligent response.

"Without question," Jack said. "I'm confident that given compliance with the Right Clients/Right Terms℠ criteria, a successful Transition Meeting, and a good start up, your company will solve the client's problems. And, based on the deals you're doing today (which, by the way, are very different than the straight 'fee-for-service' deals that were typical when I started with the company), you'll increase your fees. I'm absolutely confident that at some point in the future, most of your contracts will look like the illustration I drew for you."

"And then if our client's management changes, we're in trouble?" Bonnie asked.

"Well," Jack responded, "as you know from the work we've done before, *When people change, everything has the potential to change.*"

"That's the truth," Bonnie agreed.

"But I think there's much more to it than that."

"What do you mean?"

"Let's look at the illustration one more time," Jack said. "We looked at it from the client's point of view a little while ago; now let's look at it from your point of view. What do you see in Year 1?"

Why Good Clients
Fire
Great Companies

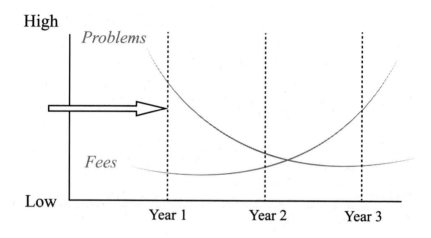

"Well. . . I see us doing what we were hired to do: solving the client's problems."

"Agreed. Are you being adequately compensated for that effort?"

"No." Bonnie acknowledged. "Not in Year 1, especially if we've been awarded the bid based on an RFP. Competition always forces skinny margins. You know that. But we'll make money in the later years because, as you said earlier, we are good at what we do."

"But, as Gambra is teaching us, we may not always be around long enough to do that," Jack observed.

Not wanting to dwell on the Gambra situation, he continued quickly: "It seems to me that when our company started in this business years ago, things were a lot simpler. Essentially, we supplied a management service for a fee. But over the years, in response to changes in our customers' situations and, I must admit, to competitive pressures, we've taken on more and more risk—in the sense that we now tie our compensation to performance targets, efficiency benchmarks, or satisfaction scores, all the while delivering the services within tighter and tighter budgets. Right?"

"That's all true. The market has changed dramatically, and the way our compensation is structured has changed, as well," Bonnie replied.

"You called it 'compensation,'" Jack continued. "I don't understand how you can call it that in this new evironment when you can invest tens—if not hundreds—of thousands of

Why Good Clients
Fire
Great Companies

dollars in start-up expenses during the initial phases of our contracts with no guarantee that we'll have the opportunity to earn a return on those investments."

"But we do," Bonnie insisted. "It just takes us time to turn an operation around. Once we do, as you've indicated in your 'Year 3,' we make a very fair return on those investments."

"But what happens if we never get to Year 3?"

This was a question Bonnie hadn't anticipated.

"Like with Gambra," she conceded, realizing the significance of Jack's point.

"Exactly. If you never get to Year 3, you never get 'compensated,' and all your work is for nothing—or very little—unless I'm missing something."

"But, Jack," Bonnie said defensively, "that's just the way our industry works. Every one of our competitors bids this way. If we were to structure a proposal that compensated us for the work we do in the early years of the contract, we'd never get any new business. Look at it from the client's point of view. Why would anyone pay a company more if a competitor is willing to do the same job for less?"

"You're right," Jack agreed. "They'd be foolish to do that. But it's not a question of paying *more*; it's a question of paying *differently*. Just look at the illustration."

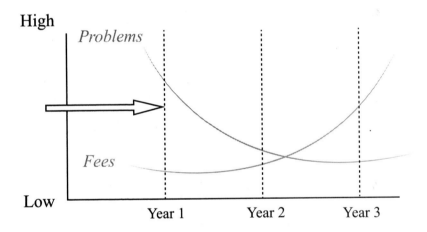

Jack explained: "You're solving the client's problems early in the contract, but you're undercompensated for those achievements. Then, in later years, you're being overcompensated for the work that's being delivered; so it's

Why Good Clients
Fire
Great Companies

just a matter of getting the compensation to match the effort and resources expended. You'll make the same, and your clients will pay the same, but the timing of the payments will more closely match the services performed and the improvements delivered."

"Jack, it's hard to argue with what you're saying, and if I could wave a magic wand and change the way the industry operates, I would," Bonnie declared. "What you're suggesting is logical, but I'm afraid our industry has never been accused of succumbing to logic."

"I see," Jack said, looking at Bonnie. "Mind if I ask you a couple of questions about industry practices?"

"Here we go!" she thought, smiling to herself.

"Think back with me, Bonnie," Jack began. "Let's pretend we're taking a trip in Mr. Peabody's WayBack machine."

Bonnie chuckled as she thought of Jack's growing penchant for using analogies from Saturday morning TV. This one, from *The Adventures of Rocky and Bullwinkle*, involved travel in a time machine. Clearly Jack, a doting grandpa, now spent way too much time watching cartoons with his increasing number of grand babies. But since Bonnie herself was a longtime fan of Mr. Peabody and Sherman, she played right along.

"Okay, where should we set the date?"

"Let's go back in time—back when the industry was just beginning to change from using a predominantly fee-based compensation structure to using the 'risk-oriented' compensation structures so prevalent today."

"All right. . . I'm there."

"Do you remember what was behind the changes in compensation and deal structure?"

"I think so, but I may need a little help filling in the gaps. After all, that was right in the middle of your heyday."

"You start, and I'll do all I can to help. The memory is fading fast, though." Jack flashed a small smile in Bonnie's direction.

Why Good Clients
Fire
Great Companies

"Well, as I've heard it, our firm was happy with the way things were in those days. We were the acknowledged leaders in the industry, our reputation was solid, and clients sought us out for our expertise."

"I'm with you so far," Jack concurred.

"Fee-for-service seemed like a fair way to price our contracts. We had the expertise, systems, and support structure to solve our clients' problems. The fees were fair for the results delivered. Life was good," Bonnie concluded.

"But, as we've talked about so many times in the past," Jack interjected, "markets are always changing. Competitors are always looking for an edge—an advantage."

"Yes, and, if I have the history right, it was our largest competitor that introduced the 'risk' or 'pay-for-performance' mentality to the industry," Bonnie agreed. "We were taking market share from them because of our superior systems, and they had to find a way to compete, knowing they were years behind us in development."

"Let me add," Jack said, "their initial decision to enter into a 'risk' contract may not have been premeditated. I don't want to give them that much credit for strategic thinking! If memory serves, our clients were all beginning to experience economic pressures because of the changes in our industry. As much as our competitors were looking for a 'hook,' I think it was the clients who forced everyone to do business differently. Remember, although it's business as usual today, back then all of this 'short-term' orientation, of making the month and quarter—forget what happens in the long term—was brand new. Sakes alive! How things have changed."

Jack was feeling his age for the first time in a while. "Clients used to stay in place. People remained with companies for their entire careers. They knew that the decisions they made today generated the results they'd have to live with in the years to come."

"And loyalty used to mean something," Bonnie added. "It certainly doesn't mean as much as it used to. In many cases it means nothing at all."

"No, it doesn't," Jack agreed. "And the defections started back then, when the competition initiated 'risk-sharing proposals' as a way to differentiate themselves from us. Since they hadn't made the investments in the infrastructure and couldn't deliver the results we could with any degree of consistency, they promised what the clients wanted to hear—

Why Good Clients
Fire
Great Companies

with little consideration of the consequences, I might add."

"And did it ever work!" Bonnie exclaimed, well aware of the distress these conditions had caused within her company. "They took contract after contract from us. No matter how much we preached about the long-term benefits that clients would realize from outsourcing their departments to us, our sales efforts fell on deaf ears. . ." Bonnie's voice trailed off.

"You're exactly right," Jack confirmed. "Superior systems or services didn't matter to clients. Better people didn't matter to clients. Long-term, sustainable improvements didn't matter either. It was simply a question of 'How much will you do, how little will it cost, and how will you *guarantee* your results?' I remember the late-night meetings, the debates, and the anguish that took place at the senior management level of our company as we pondered our response. Frankly, some of us were adamant in wanting to 'no bid' these kinds of contracts. Even then we anticipated what you're experiencing today. In fact, the sketches I shared with you earlier are the same ones we used to make our points."

"So these insights into the Gambra situation didn't occur to you this morning," Bonnie replied with relief.

Why Good Clients
Fire
Great Companies

"Far from it!" Jack assured her. "I've been concerned about this for longer than we've known each other."

"Then why did we ever follow the competition?"

"Because the ownership of our company decided to take the firm public," he explained. "Our initial stock offering was already in the works. Our underwriters had built a lot of momentum, and the market was waiting for the stock to come out. The underwriters were revising the initial asking price upward on a weekly basis. The concern—and it was real— was that if we did anything to cause a hiccup in top-line growth, our stock price would suffer. A lot of very influential people were going to be more than a little upset. The pressure was for growth, and growth at any cost."

He continued: "To be honest, the chairman expressed his reservations to me. But he felt he had no choice; he had to keep the sales coming in. That's the lure of money, I guess."

"There's been an upside to it all, though," Bonnie offered.

"And that would be?"

Why Good Clients
Fire
Great Companies

"Well, once our firm realized that *our* profits were at stake and there wasn't a guaranteed margin like there is in fee-based contracts, the culture of our organization changed for the better in that we began to really focus on our clients' operations. If we were to do a 'before and after' analysis, I think you'd find that we react to client needs more quickly than when we operated under a fee arrangement. It became clear that we had to run each client's operation as if it were our own. In fact, Jack, *running the client's operation as if it were our own* became the eleventh principle of client retention within the company. See, I've added it to the ten I inherited from you." Bonnie pulled a laminated card from the portfolio she always carried.

Jack looked at the card containing the commandments that had served him so well

Commandments of Client Retention

1. Client retention begins with the right clients under the right terms.

2. Start the contract according to the client's expectations.

3. Expect your clients to have expectations you didn't think they would have.

4. Always protect your client's interests.

5. Client retention is not an event, it is a daily process.

6. When people change, everything has the potential to change.

7. Keep track of past clients throughout their careers.

8. The worst time to renew a contract is when it is due for renewal.

9. The end of a contract doesn't have to mean the end of a relationship.

10. How you close a contract is just as important as how you open one.

11. Run the client's operation as if it were your own.

"Nice addition."

"Thanks, Jack," Bonnie replied. "The 'guaranteed contract' has given our organization a new sense of urgency. It's been good for all of us."

Why Good Clients
Fire
Great Companies

"In every cloud, a silver lining, huh?"

"Something like that. But let's get back to today," Bonnie suggested. "The fact is that Gambra has canceled. Thanks to your analysis, and these sketches, and the discussion we've had, I understand things better, and I appreciate what may be going through the new CEO and CFO's minds. But where does that leave us?"

"Well, let's take one more look at the last sketch. What's missing in Year 3 from the client's point of view?" Jack asked.

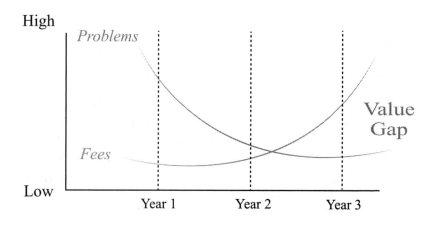

Why Good Clients
Fire
Great Companies

Bonnie looked at the drawing and the truth hit her full force: "*Value!*" she exclaimed.

"Exactly," Jack said, smiling at her revelation.

"Wait a minute, Jack, this drawing can't be right." Bonnie suddenly questioned her own insight.

"Why not?"

"Because we're providing a boatload of value to the client."

"Really?"

"Absolutely."

"Like what?"

"Well, among other things, we provide managers for their operations, oversight through our district and regional support teams, and buying power for their supplies and materials. They could never duplicate the clout we provide through our national purchasing agreements. We manage payables and cash flow on their behalf, we manage hundreds of their employees, we share fiscal responsibility for the

Why Good Clients *Fire* Great Companies

performance of their operations—guaranteeing performance—which, by the way, their own managers in other departments don't do. And we're carrying tens of thousands in receivables. That's a lot of value!" Bonnie concluded with more than a hint of satisfaction in her voice.

"But," Jack asked, confronting her mildly but decisively, "is it Relevant Value to the client?"

It's All About
Relevant Value

Why Good Clients
Fire
Great Companies

"What do you mean by Relevant Value?" Bonnie demanded of Jack, her exasperation increasing by the minute. "Value is value, isn't it?"

"I'm not so sure," he responded. "Let me explain. Since I left the firm, I've had a chance to do some thinking about what we do and why. I haven't discussed these ideas with anyone else, so I'd appreciate it if you'd listen with an open mind and tell me if I'm off base."

"Okay," Bonnie took a sip of coffee. "You haven't disappointed me yet."

"Where to begin?" Jack asked, half to himself. "Okay, when you're inside our company, it's easy to get caught up in all the things we provide for our clients. All the things you mentioned earlier are the essence of what and who we think we are. We're managers—both on-site and over-site. We're our knowledge base, our systems, our national agreements, and our proprietary intellectual property. Right?"

"I agree so far," Bonnie concurred.

"And we've spent years and millions of dollars developing those capabilities, haven't we?"

"Yes. . . and?"

"Well, having been on the outside for a time, I can see that because we've spent millions on things, and they're important to us, we tend to believe they must be equally important to our clients."

"Jack, I'm listening, but I have no clue where you're headed with this. We don't invent systems or invest in resources for the hell of it. As you know, just about every feature we add stems from a documented client need or a competitive threat. In fact, we conduct thorough market research before we make most of our significant investments."

"I know, and I'm not taking issue with *why* we develop capabilities or invest in resources. But I am taking issue with our desire to have clients perceive those investments as something that delivers value to them."

Bonnie couldn't even get out a "huh?" She stared blankly at Jack.

"I can see I haven't connected with you," he said.

Why Good Clients
Fire
Great Companies

"You could say that! Why shouldn't we expect the clients to see value in our investments and capabilities? After all, we made those investments in response to *their* needs."

"I'm not debating that point; but in my opinion, there comes a time when each client no longer sees a specific resource as 'relevant' and the value of that resource is diminished. Whether it's due to the Expectations Paradox[sm] that we both believe in or something else, I'm not quite sure. But I do know it happens.

"Let me give you an example," Jack continued, realizing that Bonnie hadn't yet bought in.

"Please."

"Well, let's use something that you cited as 'value' just a moment ago. You mentioned that through our national purchasing agreements, we give Gambra buying power the organization could never duplicate on its own. Right?"

"Right. Because of our size and scope, our purchasing leverage is significant, and we provide cash flow for the materials. The float is about forty-five days. That's a little longer than the terms of the contract, but we don't get too upset about it as long as Gambra reimburses us consistently."

"Okay," Jack continued, "let me ask you: How do you know the client still finds this leverage *relevant* enough for you to use it as part of your 'value' justification in retaining the contract?"

"Gambra wouldn't be able to purchase materials at the same level of efficiency or cost effectiveness without us, that's how."

"Really?"

"Really! You know that's true, Jack. I've heard you say the same things to clients dozens of times."

"You're right; I have. But I may have been wrong. Let me explain why: from the glance I took at Gambra's financials this morning, I'd say they're doing a little over $3 million in annual purchasing. Right?"

"Actually, the number will be closer to $4 million because of some new initiatives slated for the fourth quarter of the year."

"Okay, at $4 million, what kind of rebates are we earning from the suppliers?"

Why Good Clients
Fire
Great Companies

"I'm not exactly sure. You know how protective the purchasing group is of those numbers. But considering the offsets to our costs the division received last year when we closed the books, it looks like we're making about 6 percent.

"So, that's about a quarter of a million dollars flowing to our bottom line?"

"Yes. But if you're going to suggest that we shouldn't be taking those rebates, or that we should be passing them along to our clients, this is going to be a very long discussion."

"Bonnie, that's a debate unto itself. I'm not going there," Jack assured her. "What I am suggesting is that in this Internet age, and with the development of regional, national, and industry-specific purchasing groups—along with Gambra's size—it just may be that they no longer 'need' our purchasing expertise like they once did. The fact is, in Gambra's case, our purchasing capabilities may no longer provide enough Relevant Value to help protect the contract."

"You're saying that thanks to structural changes in the market and Gambra's situation, they can do for themselves what, once upon a time, only we could do for them?"

Why Good Clients
Fire
Great Companies

"Exactly!" Jack replied, quickly adding, "That's not to say we still can't purchase better than they can. But is the *difference* significant enough to make it *relevant* in keeping the contract?"

"Our purchasing power is one of the cornerstones of our company, Jack. If you're suggesting it no longer provides a competitive advantage, we're in trouble—deep trouble."

"That's not what I'm saying at all. Our purchasing expertise is, and hopefully will continue to be, a key competitive distinction and advantage. What I am suggesting is that after a time, it may not provide Relevant Value *to a particular client*. And when you look at it from Gambra's point of view, our purchasing power is only relevant in what it does for *them*, regardless of what we're able to save our 'average' client."

"Jack," Bonnie said, "I need a few minutes to think. If what you've just said is true, then we have to rethink our strategies for retaining our clients."

"'Rethink' might be too strong a word. 'Refine' might be a better label for what needs to happen," Jack reassured her. He continued: "Given the luxury of thirty years' experience and

Why Good Clients
Fire
Great Companies

now with retirement time to reflect on it, I really think this is
one of the most important concepts I've learned, even though
I haven't been able to articulate it until now. Relevant Value
has always been our secret weapon in making us different
from our competitors. The Clients for Life client-retention
process had us practicing it all along; we just didn't know
what to call it."

As always when Jack was expounding on an idea vital to the
Clients for Life philosophy, he grew more and more excited.
"When you really think about it," he went on, "other
companies make client presentations that say, 'Here's who
we are, here's what we do, here's how it will benefit you,
here's who else we do this for—wouldn't you agree we're
great?' Even more amazing, they actually train their account
management people in selling strategies and persuasive
selling techniques to get clients to agree with their
propaganda. What a crock!

"But because we base *our* client-management practices on
the bedrock principle of understanding and delivering on our
clients' expectations, we can ensure that the value we provide
is relevant to the way *they* measure the success of the
relationship."

Why Good Clients
Fire
Great Companies

"I'm going to need a minute or two to digest this," Bonnie replied.

"Let's take fifteen. I'm sure the rest of the world hasn't stopped while we've been talking," Jack said ruefully. "Why don't you check messages and see what else Lindsey has for you?"

At Bonnie's grateful nod, he suggested, "While you're catching up with the rest of your life, let me put some thoughts on the whiteboard in the conference room. As I've been saying, I've had a lot of time to think lately. I've been playing with approaches to understanding Relevant Value in relation to a particular client, and I'd like to get your reaction."

"Go for it! I'll be back in fifteen," Bonnie said, feeling better after having met with Jack, but still uncertain of how to retain Gambra's business. "A.J. should be here in a little while."

"Great," Jack affirmed. " I'll meet you in the conference room."

Why Good Clients
Fire
Great Companies

Three Perspectives

Why Good Clients
Fire
Great Companies

As Bonnie walked toward her office, Jack knew he'd just added to her anxiety. He sensed that she didn't yet understand the link between their conversation on Relevant Value and the action she needed to take with Gambra Incorporated. He also knew that she had to be feeling the pressure of the pending phone call to Gambra's CEO.

Jack decided to take Bonnie and A.J. through the logic he'd wrestled with as he first hypothesized the notion of Relevant Value. Moving to the whiteboard in the conference room, he began to write the elements of a process he believed would help Bonnie and A.J. decide which components of their company's service package would continue to provide Relevant Value to Gambra Incorporated. Obviously, if Gambra's senior managers didn't feel they were receiving value from the association with Service Enterprises, Bonnie and A.J. would be unlikely to retain the business.

On the board, Jack wrote...

Why Good Clients
Fire
Great Companies

Relevant Value

Understanding Relevant Value is necessary

- to identify and segment the critical components of the service offered

- to understand the relationship of those components from three distinct points of view:

  - from the client's current perspective

  - from our current perspective

  - from an ideal perspective—with client retention as the singular goal

- to specifically identify the major service components that would be most painful for the client to lose if the contract was canceled

- to create a client communication strategy that allows us to influence the client's perspective regarding the source of the value they receive

Why Good Clients
Fire
Great Companies

As Jack wrote the last sentence on the board, he found himself reviewing the rationale he would use if Bonnie or A.J. asked him to explain his thinking.

"One of the things that has always frustrated me," he thought, "was how clients so often based their opinion of the company on the specific performance of the account manager and, to a lesser extent, the on-site account team.

"We all understand how important those individuals are, but clients seem to give very little thought to the system under which the account manager or team operates.

"Service Enterprises starts by recruiting better people because we have better recruiters. We train them better because we have better trainers. We mentor them better because our senior managers are dedicated to it. We provide them varied and useful job experiences because we have a diverse client base that allows us to do so. We support them with enlightened regional managers because we have tremendous depth in our system. Finally, we equip them with the best systems, ideas, and targeted innovations, all of which have been tested and benchmarked.

Why Good Clients
Fire
Great Companies

"Yet what do we hear? It's all about the account manager. If we allow or, Heaven forbid, encourage our clients to think this way, the value they perceive from our company may become dangerously out of sync with the *real* source of the value they receive.

"When you think of it, our ability to retain clients would be enhanced if clients perceived much *lower* value in the individual account manager. As important as the account manager is, we want client firms to prize the overriding relationship with our entire organization and *not* the relationship with any individual. It's up to us to help them understand that we have management talent available at every level and that the *true source of the value they receive* lies in the fact that we can replace managers without a hiccup in performance.

"When it comes to changing client perceptions of our involvement," Jack told himself, "we really need to concentrate on two issues: selectiveness and communication. First, the simple fact is, not everything we do is relevant to every client. Second, communicating and showing how the value we deliver meets the client's current needs is what puts us in the strongest position to retain the business.

Why Good Clients
Fire
Great Companies

"It's our job to help clients understand what *really* allows them to experience the value they derive from the association with Service Enterprises. If we can't, we deserve the consequences."

Realizing that the morning had slipped away, Jack didn't wait for Bonnie and A.J. to brainstorm a list of their company's key service components. The list Jack placed on the whiteboard wasn't exhaustive, but he felt it contained the service components that really mattered. He wrote, in no particular order of importance

Key Service Components

	Client's Perspective	Our Perspective	Ideal
1. On-site management			
2. Regional management/oversight			
3. Purchasing power			
4. Cost guarantees			
5. Proprietary systems			
6. Management stability/recruiting			
7. HR administration			
8. High-level entertainment			
9. Expert knowledge			
10. Integrated services			

Why Good Clients
Fire
Great Companies

Below the key service components, Jack wrote the four strategic questions he believed critical to retaining the Gambra Incorporated contract:

1. Gambra hired us because. . .
2. Gambra will renew our contract only if. . .
3. If Gambra cancels our contract, the major thing they lose is. . .
4. The *one thing* we need to do to retain Gambra's business is. . .

"You look like one of my old professors up there at the board," A.J. called out as he entered the room.

"A.J.! How have you been, young man?" Jack asked with sincere affection.

Even though the two hadn't seen one another recently, their mutual feelings of respect and admiration were obvious.

"Great, until late yesterday," A.J. replied.

"Keep everything in perspective," Jack advised in a fatherly tone, shaking A.J.'s hand.

"Easier said than done," A.J. said softly. "What's all this?" he continued, taking in Jack's handiwork.

Why Good Clients
Fire
Great Companies

"A little something I'd like to discuss with you and Bonnie. I'm hoping it'll help us with the Gambra situation."

"We need all the help we can get. By the way, I stopped by Bonnie's office on my way in. She said she'd be here in five minutes."

"Good. That'll give us a chance to cover a couple of things."

As A.J. settled into one of the chairs at the conference table, Jack caught his eye. "I reviewed some of the Gambra files earlier today and I didn't see the Transition Lite report from the meetings with the new CEO and CFO," Jack said, hiding his concern.

"I have 'em right here," A.J. reached for his briefcase. "I took them home last night. I wanted to go over them again, just to be sure I hadn't missed anything."

"That's my boy!" Jack thought to himself, becoming convinced A.J. had complied with all of the Clients for Life requirements and that his resignation, and those of his managers, would only go one place—the trash can.

"Anything jump out at you?" he asked, scanning the documents.

Why Good Clients
Fire
Great Companies

"Nada. . . Shoot! I still can't believe this!" A.J. nearly shouted, his frustration and disappointment bubbling to the surface. Then, taking a deep breath, he began to explain what had transpired. "We met, we followed the Transition Lite protocol, we successfully communicated the value we had provided in the past, we discussed their expectations, and I thought we reached consensus that we were on the right track. They seemed genuinely pleased with our management style, our priorities, and the financial and operational condition of the account. I thought we did a good job of acknowledging the new leadership at Gambra and establishing that we were prepared to help them succeed.

"As you probably saw in the notes," A.J. continued, "we discussed the CFO's request for an additional 20 percent reduction in their overall costs. We told her that with the current resources and budget they'd allocated to the operation, it would be next to impossible to deliver on that expectation."

"How did she react?"

"Initially, she seemed frustrated with us, but we used their own numbers to prove we'd be unlikely to achieve that level of savings in the majority of their operations. In fact, while we committed to deliver 30 percent reductions from their new acquisitions, we made it clear that we'd be lucky to offset inflationary increases at the facilities we've managed on their behalf since the beginning of the contract. As you know, Jack, we've managed some of those facilities for years. There's not a lot of costs left to wring out of those operations. The net result is that we committed to a 7 percent overall reduction."

"And?" Jack prodded.

"She studied the numbers, she asked some questions about the last couple of quarters' performance, and she said she'd think about what we'd told her."

"What was the CEO's response?"

"To tell you the truth, he couldn't have been more agreeable. Didn't have one question. He said we were doing a great job. He even said—and I'm quoting now—he 'wished all his departments were as well run as the ones we managed.'"

"Always nice when that happens. Let's get back to the CFO. Knowing you, A.J., I can't imagine the conversation ended there."

Why Good Clients
Fire
Great Companies

A.J. smiled. "You're right. It would have been suicide to let something like that fester. Naturally, we confirmed her expectations and our commitments in writing. After a week or so, I called to schedule a follow-up meeting. I suggested that we talk further about her expectation that we deliver a 20 percent reduction in overall costs. I said it was important for her to be comfortable with our position and explanation. If there were any unresolved questions or concerns, I wanted to get them out on the table."

"Anything come of it?"

"We met and talked again about the numbers we'd presented. She asked a couple of questions about staffing in some of the operations, and then we talked about the structure of our contract."

"Oh?" Jack's interest was piqued by A.J.'s last statement.

"Yeah," A.J. confirmed. "She couldn't quite understand our invoices or why we were billing Gambra at the current levels. Before you ask, Jack," A.J. said preemptively, "I taught her how to interpret our invoices, and I reviewed the terms of the contract with her."

Why Good Clients
Fire
Great Companies

"And she was satisfied?" Jack asked, still a little concerned about what he'd just heard.

"Seemed to be," A.J. replied. "Although it was written a while ago, the contract language is pretty straightforward—unlike the gobbledygook we put in contracts today. We discussed the whole 'pay-for-performance' philosophy, as well as the impact Gambra's client-satisfaction scores had on our ability to max our compensation."

Then, almost as an afterthought, A.J. added, "She said it was the first time she'd been exposed to this type of contract. But she admitted that we seemed to be doing an excellent job and earning the money Gambra was paying us."

Before Jack could voice his next question, A.J. plunged on, "I wanted to be sure there weren't any lingering concerns. So when Bonnie went in for her initial Web-rebuilding visit about six months ago, I asked her to bring it up again. I think her notes from the meeting are in the T.A.R.P folder."

As A.J. mentioned the T.A.R.P form, Jack realized that Bonnie had interrupted his T.A.R.P review earlier in the morning.

Why Good Clients
Fire
Great Companies

"Let me take a look," Jack said to A.J., reaching for the Team Account Retention Plan folder once more.

"I'm going to grab a Coke while you look it over, Jack. I want to be settled in when Bonnie gets here. Can I bring you anything?"

"No, thanks. Any more caffeine and I'll be lucky to write in a straight line."

"Okay, I'll be right back," A.J. called over his shoulder as he headed out the door.

But Jack never heard him. Before A.J. was halfway down the hall, Jack had found what he was looking for. Bonnie's notes in the T.A.R.P. folder read: *"New CFO has no experience with management companies. Concerned about her interpretation of our contract. Isn't seeing the big picture. Only focused on what they're paying us—not on what we're providing.*

I think I've overcome her concerns by emphasizing that we get paid only if we perform—that their costs of operation are guaranteed and our compensation is tied to client satisfaction.

Be sure to review with A.J. and team."

This entry, coupled with what A.J. had just told him, sent a chill down Jack's spine.

Why Good Clients
Fire
Great Companies

Four Questions

Why Good Clients
Fire
Great Companies

Jack sat in a daze, thoughts racing through his head. "It's here—right here," he kept saying to himself. "Bonnie and A.J. must realize it."

As he rhythmically tapped his knee with the T.A.R.P. folder, Jack took a deep breath, gathered himself, and said out loud, "I know Bonnie. I know she realizes how important this is or she would never have written it down! Why hasn't she said anything about her concerns regarding the CFO's experience or perceptions?"

This situation reminded Jack of why, during his tenure as vice president of ops, he insisted that notes be taken at every client meeting and sent to his office immediately after. During the course of a year, there might be forty or fifty separate entries transferred to the T.A.R.P. folder from managers within the Web of Influence. Individually, these observations might not cause concern; but when linked together, they often indicated something that could threaten the relationship.

If the administrative assistant had done her job—and Jack's always had—the T.A.R.P. folder contained every entry, all the insights. That's why, in Bonnie's words, it was his "go to" form.

Why Good Clients
Fire
Great Companies

As Jack and Rosemary, his wife of forty-three years, often found when solving crossword puzzles together, a handful of words seemed to hold the key. Once they identified those key words, everything else would fall into place. In Jack's experience, the same principle applied to the comments in the T.A.R.P. folder. A few observations usually provided the insights necessary to protect the contract.

Jack now had to decide how to confront Bonnie and A.J. with one of the keys to the Gambra Incorporated cancellation. But he wondered how they both could have missed the magnitude of such obvious factors as the CFO's lack of experience with outsourcing partners and her concerns about compensation.

He knew how tense they were. Bonnie certainly didn't need the additional stress of being reproached. And while A.J. put up a brave front, he was equally fragile at this moment. Besides, Jack thought, his own conclusions could be way off base. Increasingly, though, he didn't think so. He knew that being removed from an emotional situation allowed a certain clarity of thought.

Everything considered, Jack decided that rather than confront Bonnie and A.J. directly, he'd weave his concerns about the

CFO into the conversation about Relevant Value. He wasn't quite sure how, but it seemed like the best approach at the moment.

"Hey, look who I found in the hall," A.J. called out, holding the door open for Bonnie.

Jack acknowledged them with a smile.

"I hope you don't mind," Bonnie said, "but I gave A.J. a quick briefing on what you and I covered this morning."

"Mind? I appreciate it! It'll save us a lot of time. A.J.'s not nearly as quick on the uptake as you are." Jack waited to see if A.J. would respond to the good-natured jab. "Any questions A.J.?" he asked.

"That whole idea about the value we provide being relevant is an interesting way to look at things," A.J. offered. "You know, Jack, you must really be bored if that's the kind of stuff you think about in your spare time!"

"Somebody has to do it," Jack declared, motioning A.J. and Bonnie to take their places at the conference table.

Why Good Clients
Fire
Great Companies

"Time is short," he reminded them, "so let me take you through this process. Remember, I've never shared this before, but I think it'll help prepare you to make that call this afternoon. Ready?"

"Let's do it, Big Guy," came A.J.'s prompt response.

"He'll never change," Bonnie chuckled, gesturing toward A.J.

"That's what I love about him," Jack replied.

"Okay," Jack said, drawing their attention to the board, "I've listed what I believe to be the significant components of your service package. In the old features/benefits exercises we used to do in Sales Training 101, these would be the key features. Do you have any problems with what's there? Is anything significant missing?"

A.J. and Bonnie reviewed the list and nodded their approval.

"All right, then," Jack continued, working his way to the whiteboard. "Here's what I'd like you to do. Normally, I'd ask each of you to come up with your own assessment, but because of our time constraints I'd like you to work together.

Why Good Clients
Fire
Great Companies

"You see this first column," Jack asked, pointing to the column marked "Client's Perspective."

Bonnie and A.J. nodded.

"Here's how it works," Jack began. "You each have 100 points to spend, and you must allocate them among the ten service components I've listed here. The objective is to identify which service components are the most critical— *relevant*, if you will—to Gambra's organization."

Jack paused to be certain that Bonnie and A.J. understood his instructions, then continued.

"You allocate the 100 points as if you were the CEO and CFO of Gambra Incorporated and were selecting the components that you believe offer the most value. It's critical that you do this by putting yourselves in the clients' shoes. At this point in the process, it's what *they think* that really matters. We'll get to what *you know* is important a little later.

Bonnie and A.J. began to debate which components of the service package offered the most value *from the client's point of view*. It took about fifteen minutes and a little give and take, but Bonnie eventually walked to the board and wrote down the results of their discussion.

Key Service Components

	Client's Perspective	Our Perspective	Ideal
1. On-site management	30		
2. Regional management/oversight			
3. Purchasing power	5		
4. Cost guarantees	50		
5. Proprietary systems	5		
6. Management stability/recruiting			
7. HR administration			
8. High-level entertainment			
9. Expert knowledge	10		
10. Integrated services			

"Fine," Jack said, not indicating whether he agreed or disagreed with their allocations. "Now, repeat the process, but this time under the 'Our Perspective' column, allocate the 100 points among the components on the basis of what you know *really* provides the value to Gambra's organization.

As Jack waited for Bonnie and A.J. to come to consensus, he noticed a lot more discussion between them. After at least

two trips to the board to refine their allocations, Bonnie and
A.J. indicated they were comfortable with the following
distribution:

Key Service Components

	Client's Perspective	Our Perspective	Ideal
1. On-site management	30	20	
2. Regional management/oversight		10	
3. Purchasing power	5	10	
4. Cost guarantees	50		
5. Proprietary systems	5	25	
6. Management stability/recruiting			
7. HR administration			
8. High-level entertainment			
9. Expert knowledge	10	25	
10. Integrated services		10	

"Okay," Jack said, again maintaining a neutral tone, "here's
the last thing I'd like you to do. Look at the last column, the
'Ideal' column. If we could apportion these elements to give
us the highest likelihood of retaining Gambra's business
forever, how would the percentages fall? To put it another
way, what would the ultimate 'golden handcuffs' service
package look like? What do we *want* Gambra to think?"

Why Good Clients
Fire
Great Companies

From the discussion between A.J. and Bonnie, Jack could see that this category was the toughest for them. After twenty minutes, he had to insist that they give him something they both could accept—even if they weren't in complete agreement.

"This is the best we can do without punching one another," Bonnie said in mock despair.

Key Service Components

	Client's Perspective	Our Perspective	Ideal
1. On-site management	30	20	15
2. Regional management/oversight		10	10
3. Purchasing power	5	10	20
4. Cost guarantees	50		
5. Proprietary systems	5	25	30
6. Management stability/recruiting			
7. HR administration			
8. High-level entertainment			
9. Expert knowledge	10	25	15
10. Integrated services		10	10

Why Good Clients
Fire
Great Companies

"Let's take a look at what you think is going on from the three unique perspectives," Jack suggested, once again moving to the front of the room.

"You seem to feel the clients believe the real value is in the guarantees provided by the company. If I'm correct, what you think they say to themselves is, 'Gambra really has no downside. As long as the numbers are guaranteed and the internal level of satisfaction with the service is acceptable, we don't need to know much more about anything.'"

"Well," A.J. replied, "we believe they think the on-site manager is important, and they give us credit for knowing our stuff. But," he continued with a sigh, "as long as we guarantee the number and their people are happy with us, they couldn't care less. All the other stuff is sort of 'behind the scenes' to them. As you say Jack, it isn't *relevant*."

"But," Bonnie interjected, "as you can see from 'Our Perspective,' we know it's *really* our proprietary systems that give us the ability to drive lower costs—it's only because of those systems that we're able to *guarantee* cost reductions."

Before Jack could respond, Bonnie continued. "Sure, our on-site management is a crucial component of the service mix.

Why Good Clients
Fire
Great Companies

"That manager is the one who accesses the company's expert knowledge. In essence, he or she is the conduit between the company's expertise and the client's operation. We know how critical it is to have the right manger at the right account. Nothing happens without that."

"And, as you know, Jack," A.J. chimed in, "my role as part of the regional support is to expand and help manage the Web of Influence. If we're not connected within the client's organization at levels the on-site manager can't get to, we might miss key pieces of information that can help better manage and protect the account."

Jack nodded his agreement as A.J. went on. "It's up to me and the rest of the support staff to integrate all of our systems within the account—to look at the bigger strategic picture, and share the learning that we have acquired from other contracts we manage. The on-site manager's responsibility is to deal with the tactical day-to-day issues and opportunities."

"Okay," Jack responded. "I understand what you believe the clients think provides Relevant Value to them. I also understand your sense of 'reality.' And, by the way, I don't disagree with anything you've said. But before we can discuss how we're going to create the 'ideal' situation—a situation that'll make it much more difficult for Gambra's CEO and CFO to walk away—I need a few more pieces of information." Without a hint of apology, he added, "I'll need to introduce a concept that may be difficult for you to accept."

Before Bonnie and A.J. could respond to this last assertion, Jack asked them to address the first of the four questions he'd written on the whiteboard.

"How do you complete this sentence, 'Gambra hired us because. . .?'" Jack inquired.

Bonnie spoke up. "Let me answer that one. Gambra hired us because their operations were out of control—way over budget, and they'd just gone through their fourth manager in two years. The fact is, they'd tried everything they knew to get things under control, and they had failed."

"Works for me," A.J. concurred.

"Okay," Jack replied. "How about the second question, 'Gambra will renew our contract only if. . .?'"

Bonnie and A.J. stared at Jack for what seemed like ten

Why Good Clients
Fire
Great Companies

minutes before A.J. broke the silence. "My gut tells me it comes down to the 20 percent cost savings the CFO was looking for," he said.

"But, A.J.," Bonnie cut in, "you and I know that isn't possible given the current resources and budgets. The numbers are the numbers, and there's just not that much fat in their operations."

"I know that, and you know that," A.J. replied. "But Jack is asking something else. He wants to know what it will take for Gambra to renew the contract. I think the 20 percent savings is the only thing that will do it."

"Then we're going to chalk up our first loss," Bonnie replied, "'cause it ain't gonna happen."

"Do you agree with A.J.'s assessment?" Jack asked as Bonnie slumped in her chair.

"Well," she replied, "I'd have said that Gambra will renew only if we can convince them of the value we deliver. I guess A.J. and I *are* saying the same thing, but I don't see how we can increase the value by cutting their costs any more than we have."

Why Good Clients
Fire
Great Companies

All right then, it's time to step back," Jack declared. "All day
long we've talked about value and, in particular, the notion of
relevant value. In our business, value in the client's eyes is
the relationship between quality and cost, in fact,
algebraically, it looks like this:

Jack walked to the board and wrote "*Value = Quality/Cost*"

"*Cost* is straightforward, Jack continued. "It's what Gambra
pays, or, extended into the future, what they *would* pay if it
weren't for our stewardship of their operation.

"*Quality* is a little less obvious, but in our industry I suggest
that it's defined as the absence of problems combined with
the effective delivery of innovation.

"We all recognize that there are three and only three ways to
increase value: first, increase quality and keep costs the
same; second, maintain quality and decrease costs—which,
by the way is what Gambra is asking us to do—; and third,
increase quality and decrease costs.

"Bonnie, do you remember your concerns regarding the CFO
and the notes you made in the T.A.R.P. form?"

Why Good Clients
Fire
Great Companies

At Bonnie's nod, Jack continued: "Thinking back to that conversation and the concept of value, specifically as it is relevant to the CFO's world, what's your reaction to what I just put on the board?"

"Well," Bonnie replied, "I didn't feel the CFO really understood how the numbers came together. Value wasn't working for her because she couldn't quantify the 'cost' factor in the value equation."

"Do you still have those concerns?" Jack asked.

"To be honest, Jack, I don't—or I didn't. I thought A.J.'s follow-up meetings and my conversation with her and the new CEO covered their concerns, especially about our compensation. Obviously, I was mistaken."

"Don't beat yourself up," Jack urged.

"Ahh, Jack," Bonnie sighed. "I've gone over and over those meetings in my mind. I know I had concerns when I left, but I thought we'd covered them. I was confident they'd recognize the value we're delivering, just as their predecessors had. When I met the CEO, he was so complimentary of our management of the operation, I guess I got a little overconfident—even complacent. Looking back, I guess I convinced myself that the CFO's lack of familiarity with management services was behind her concerns and not her issues about the costs. Why didn't I *listen*?"

"You did, Bonnie," A.J. replied. "You listened well. *I* was the one who told you not to worry because I had dealt with the CFO's concerns. *I* was the one who said, 'She understands why we're making the amount we are for what we do, even if she initially felt it was 'too much.' *I* was the one who—"

"Hold it!" Jack admonished. "We can go over the lessons learned tonight, after Bonnie calls the CEO. We're in this together, A.J. Don't forget that."

Realizing he'd heard what he needed to hear about Bonnie's notations in the T.A.R.P. folder, Jack continued. "How about the third question, 'If Gambra Incorporated cancels our contract today, the major thing they lose is. . .?'"

A.J. and Bonnie's enthusiastic response reminded Jack of an auction, their words flying so fast he couldn't understand a syllable. All three colleagues chuckled at Bonnie and A.J.'s eagerness to share what Gambra would lose by canceling the contract.

Why Good Clients
Fire
Great Companies

"Ladies before gentlemen," A.J. said, leaning back in his chair and smiling at Bonnie.

Bonnie smiled back. "The major thing they'd lose is our systems," she said. "Without those systems in place, it won't be twelve months before their costs begin to go up—and quickly. They've relied on us for years. I don't even think they've thought about what they'd have to recreate if we left."

"Do you agree?" Jack asked A.J.

"I do, but I can't help thinking that losing our management team would be a huge blow to them, as well. Karen and her staff really know the operation, and they have excellent rapport with Gambra's managers. Besides, when it comes to integrating our systems into client operations, no one in the region is better than Karen."

"Great," Jack said, "I'll accept both answers. Both would be major losses to Gambra. What about question number four, 'The one thing we need to do to retain Gambra Incorporated's business is…?'"

"I need a few minutes to think about that one," A.J. said.

Bonnie nodded her agreement.

"No problem," Jack responded. "Take all the time you need."

With that, the room fell silent. Jack made a few notes to himself as he watched A.J. and Bonnie ponder this question.

Finally, Bonnie spoke up. "At the risk of being redundant," she began, "I think we have to show them what would happen to the operation without our management. Their ongoing costs of operation would go up significantly within a year. Finding a new management team and replacing our systems would impact their short-term costs. And, while they were replacing the team and systems, their efficiency would tumble. With all that going on, there's no way they'd come close to saving the 20 percent the CFO is looking for. In fact, I'd be shocked if their costs didn't go up—even after they factored in 'saving' the fees we're paid for managing the operation."

"I agree and disagree," A.J. offered. "I agree that their continuing costs of operation would increase. I also agree they would have a hard time replacing our managers and systems. But I don't think they'd suffer short-term inefficiencies."

Why Good Clients *Fire* Great Companies

"Help me understand why," Bonnie said.

"Because you know as well as I do that if they decided to cancel, we'd transition appropriately. We wouldn't let them struggle. We'd stay on board until they were up and running with their new team. Even though we haven't had a client cancel in a long, long time, we've all agreed to live by the principles of the Clients for Life client-retention process. Number Ten is: *How you close an account is just as important as how you start one.* And we'd close it right. We owe that to Gambra, no matter what they decide," A.J. concluded.

"You're right, A.J. I do know that as well as you. I guess I got carried away. It's just so frustrating to know that you're doing a great job for a good client, but they may fire you anyway."

"Tell me about it!"

"So," Jack interrupted, knowing he had to get them refocused, "The one thing you need to do to retain Gambra's business is—"

"Convince them we're the most cost-effective choice they have," Bonnie responded.

Why Good Clients
Fire
Great Companies

"I like that," A.J. agreed.

"Me, too," Jack said. "Now, there's only one more thing we have to cover before we can plan your call to Gambra's CEO. And as I said before," he cautioned, "you may not like what you're about to hear."

Why Good Clients
Fire
Great Companies

Revelation X^{sm}

As Jack moved to the board, he could feel Bonnie's and A.J.'s eyes riveted to his back.

"Let me do a quick review of something Bonnie and I discussed earlier," Jack said to A.J. He redrew the sketches he'd shared with Bonnie earlier that morning, then took A.J. through them, line by line. After fifteen minutes, A.J. was nodding as he regarded the last sketch in Jack's series.

New Client Appears

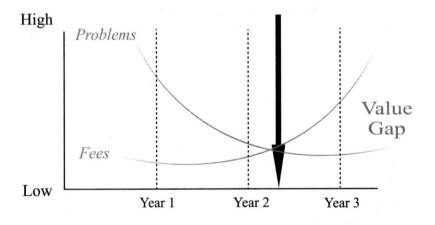

"And so," Jack said, concluding his review, "there's likely to be a significant value gap evident to the new decision-makers as they assume responsibility for the operation."

"Oh, man," A.J. moaned. "I've never even considered looking at it like that before. To think we can be in this much trouble—all because we've done what we were hired to do and lived up to the terms of the contract between the companies."

"An amazing insight, isn't it?" Bonnie shook her head.

"Yeah, but how's it gonna help us now?" A.J. asked.

"Well, there's more to Revelation X^{sm}," Jack replied.

"Revelation what?" came from A.J.

"X," Jack repeated. "I call this notion "Revelation X" because of the way the sketch looked the first time I drew it."

"You *do* have a lot of time on your hands, don't you?" A.J. laughed.

Jack enjoyed the barb, realizing that A.J.'s tension was beginning to subside. "I do," he admitted, "and I can't wait to hear your reaction to the rest of it."

Why Good Clients
Fire
Great Companies

"Shoot," A.J. replied, once again settling into his high-backed chair.

"Well," Jack began, pointing to the illustration, "what you see here *will* happen to each and every one of your accounts that has Gambra's type of contract. Not *might* happen," he emphasized, "*will* happen!

"Why?" Jack asked rhetorically. "Two reasons: first, this organization is good at what it does. You *will* solve the client's problems. Second, your compensation will go up. Everyone in this organization, from Bonnie on down, is committed to receiving a fair return for their efforts. So as the contract unfolds and reaches maturity, your compensation *will* increase as your performance improves."

"You can also bet that clients will change," Bonnie offered.

"Amen," A.J. concurred. "We're facing more client changes now than we've had in the past decade."

"And because of each of those factors, you get a situation that looks like the sketch in front of you," Jack proposed.

Revelation X

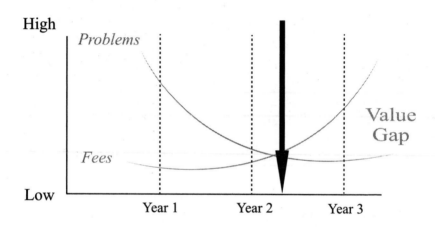

"Now, given that this is going to happen to you—that clients, especially new decision-makers, are going to see a gap in the value you're providing as the contract matures—and your responsibility is to keep 100 percent of your clients, what are you going to do?" Jack probed.

Why Good Clients *Fire* Great Companies

Bonnie and A.J. stared at the illustration.

It didn't take A.J. long to blurt out, half in jest, "I guess we have to give 'em more problems."

"Right!" came Jack's unexpected reply.

The extent of Jack's enthusiasm startled A.J.—and then confusion set in.

"Huh?" A.J. grunted. "Give 'em more problems?"

"Exactly," Jack affirmed. "Let me ask you a couple of questions."

Bonnie just smiled and watched.

"Who defines the problems at the beginning of the contract?" Jack asked, pointing to the top of the 'Problems' line in the Revelation X illustration.

"Well," A.J. said, pondering the question, "if we follow the Clients for Life client-retention process, and we always do, I imagine the answer is 'the clients.' They express their sense

Why Good Clients
Fire
Great Companies

of the problems during the Transition Meeting when they share what they expect of us."

"Exactly," Jack said again. "And you solve those problems during the life of the contract, don't you?"

"Sure. That's why they hire us," A.J. was matter-of-fact.

"Now tell me this," Jack continued as if timed by a metronome, "who are the experts in this business?"

"We are," A.J. offered.

"Right again!" Jack bellowed. "So once you've solved whatever problems your clients have described, it's time for you to educate them on problems they didn't even know they had." He drew an additional dashed line on the board to illustrate his thought.

Revelation X

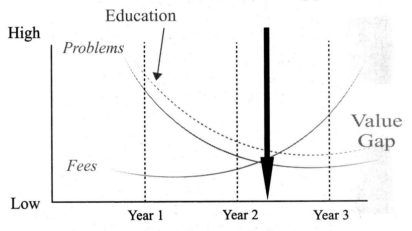

"And when you educate the client, A.J., what happens to the value gap?"

Looking at the drawing, A.J. immediately saw the impact. "It shrinks," he answered.

Why Good Clients
Fire
Great Companies

"Right. It shrinks," Jack agreed. "The client perceives more value from the services you provide."

"But that's not something new," A.J. objected. "We do that all the time. In fact, most of the issues we're working on at Gambra's locations, other than at the new acquisitions, are things they never even talked about during the Transition Meeting because it happened so long ago. If anything at all, we're responding to concerns voiced by the clients during the annual Expectations Sessions."

"I realize that," Jack replied. "Stay with me. Have you ever run out of things to 'educate' a client on?"

"You mean on our core services? Sure. As proactive as we are in delivering our technical expertise, and as much as we invest in developing innovative ways to serve our clients, there comes a time when we've done all we know how to do."

"What do you do then?" Jack persisted.

"What do you mean, what do we do then?"

"What do you do after you've delivered all you know how to

deliver in the core services the client contracted you to provide?"

"It depends," A.J. said. "In most cases, we ask 'em to give us problems to solve in other parts of their operation."

"How's that happen?" Jack asked, knowing that both he and A.J. understood the answer.

"We expand our involvement at the account by offering to provide additional services that are within our competency or by taking our core services to other parts of their operation," A.J. explained. "That's part of my regional oversight responsibility. I'm supposed to understand how to strategically bring all of our organization's competencies to bear on the client's problems, regardless of what service we provide initially."

"And when you offer to bring in additional services or assume responsibility for other departments," Jack asked, "who defines the problems?"

"We follow the same process for an 'internal' sale as we do for a 'new' sale. So I guess the answer is the same as before:

Why Good Clients
Fire
Great Companies

the clients do. They tell us what they think the problems are when they share their expectations with us at the Transition Meeting for the new service."

"So as you implement your company's processes related to the new service and eliminate those problems, it looks like this, doesn't it?" Jack asked, drawing an additional line on the board.

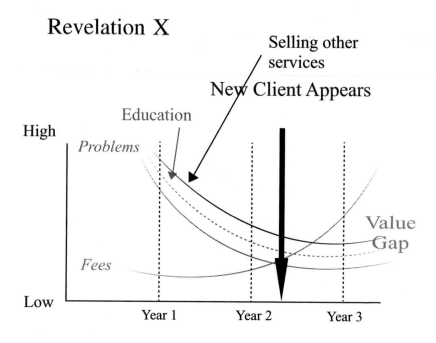

"Yes," was A.J.'s simple answer.

"And, who are the experts in those additional services?" Jack asked, certain that A.J. could see where he was headed.

"We are."

"So once again, after we solve the problems that they've identified, our job is to. . ."

"Educate them," Jack and A.J. chorused.

"And then it would look like this," A.J. continued, taking the marker from Jack and adding the appropriate dashed line to the illustration on the board.

Revelation X

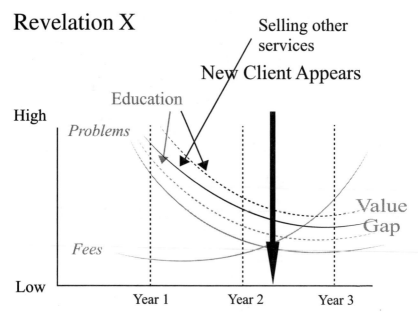

"Right," Jack agreed. "Think about it," he said to A.J. and Bonnie. "Each time you offer a new service (that is, take on additional problems for the client), you add value. Said another way, the potential value gap shrinks! So you're doing more than solving additional problems, you're capitalizing on new opportunities to build value for the client. And providing Relevant Value is not simply a matter of operating well, it's a matter of *communicating* well. In fact, great operations alone can't cut it anymore."

Why Good Clients
Fire
Great Companies

"Wow, I see why you call this a revelation," A.J. marveled.

"Notice," Jack quickly added, "I'm not saying we have to give away these services to improve the client's perception of value. As you can both see from the illustration, the fees we're receiving as illustrated here," he said, pointing to the 'Fees' line, "continue to go up."

Bonnie and A.J. nodded their agreement.

"But what happens when you run out of services to offer or departments to expand to?" Bonnie asked.

"Good question," Jack replied. "Let's look at the illustration. There are really only two lines up here, aren't there? And we've already discussed what happens to the 'Problems' line. There's only one line left."

"The 'Fees' line," Bonnie observed.

"Right," Jack agreed.

Let me ask you a question," Jack began. "Can you make too much money at an account?"

Why Good Clients
Fire
Great Companies

After a moment's reflection, Bonnie said, "Sure. Sure you can."

"How do you know when you're making too much?" Jack questioned.

"I don't know how other people 'know it,' but I just start to worry a lot," Bonnie confessed. "I worry about our competition coming in and that the clients will start to ask a lot of questions about our fees."

"Questions like Gambra's new CFO was asking?" Jack blurted out—and immediately wished he could take back his words.

"Yes, like those," Bonnie replied without rancor. "Like I said, Jack, I should have listened better."

"I'm sorry, Bonnie," Jack apologized, I didn't mean to go there."

"No harm done. Besides, you're here to help me hold up a mirror and see what happened. You don't have to worry about my feelings. My ego will survive this."

Jack smiled and knew she was right—and tough enough to deal with anything that might come along. "Okay, then, why do you worry about the competition coming in?" he asked.

"Well," Bonnie said, pointing to the board, "it's pretty clear if you look at the illustration."

"Help me," Jack encouraged.

"Let's take a look at the end of Year 2 or the beginning of Year 3 in the Revelation X diagram," Bonnie began, "in the spot after the client or clients have changed."

Bonnie moved to the board and pointed to the appropriate place on the illustration.

Revelation X

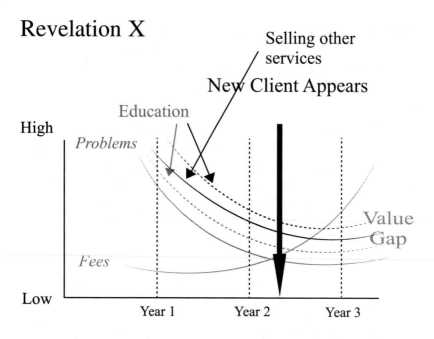

"Think about it for a moment," she continued. "We've solved the significant portion of the client's problems but haven't yet been adequately compensated for our efforts because of the deal structure. If a competitor comes in at that point, they're likely to say they can do the same thing we're doing for a lot less."

Why Good Clients
Fire
Great Companies

"Competitors can promise anything," A.J. observed.

"But it's true in this case," Bonnie challenged. "*At that point*, they *can* do what we're doing for less."

She continued: "Look at the situation. By the end of Year 2 we've *solved* most of the client's problems. What the competition sees is a relatively smooth-running operation. So they put in a bid that reflects the kind of resources they'd have to allocate to a relatively problem-free account."

"Okay, *and?*" came from A.J.

"And while the competition is putting in a low bid because they don't have to deal with a lot of the problems we had to deal with," Bonnie continued, "our fees are going up quickly because the deal structure allows us to be making that much.

"After all," she added, "at the end of Year 2 it's likely that we're only beginning to be fairly compensated for the work we did early on."

Bonnie's index finger pounded the board. "In a pay-for-performance agreement, the lion's share of our profit is built into the back end of the contract," she reminded A.J, "so while the competition is saying they'll do it for less, we're trying to justify what we're making as fair."

"But it *is* fair and we deserve it," A.J. said with conviction.

"Perhaps," Bonnie said. "Perhaps if the people who hired us were still around and we'd followed the Clients for Life client-retention process communications protocols, it might be different. But let me ask you a question," Bonnie said, realizing that she'd adopted Jack's method of teaching, "Which way do new decision-makers look when they assume responsibility for an operation? Do they look to the past, or are they interested in what happens on their watch forward?"

"They may look to the past for some perspective," A.J. offered, "but I guess it's common sense that they're concerned with what happens from the time they assume responsibility forward."

"I agree," Bonnie said. "So they don't care how many problems we had to solve or what we were compensated for our efforts. That's all in the past. What they're interested in is the most value they can get *now*. The fact is, the farther along into Year 3 we get, the tougher it's going to be to retain the contract if a competitor is asked to bid."

Why Good Clients
Fire
Great Companies

"Why is that?" A.J. wondered aloud.

"Because, once our fees start to climb, the difference between what we're making and what the competition is willing to do the same job for is exacerbated. That becomes a problem when the client shows us the competitive bid and asks us to lower our fees."

"If we lower our fees, what does that say to the client?" Bonnie asked A.J.

"I guess it says that we were making more than we should have been," A.J. answered, not quite comfortable with the notion.

"Right," Bonnie replied. "You and I both know we earned the right to make the amount stipulated in the contract—but you have to let that go or you'll never truly appreciate what Jack's sharing with us in Revelation X.

"It's clear to me now," she continued. "We may have earned what we're making at the end of Year 2, but it doesn't matter. All that matters is what's real to the *new decision-makers*. And they have a bid from a competitor that suggests we're making more than is reasonable, given the status of the operation."

Why Good Clients
Fire
Great Companies

"And if we match the bid, we've just admitted to the new decision-makers that we were charging more than we should have been," A.J. said, realizing the enormity of the implication. "If we do that, any trust we have with the clients is gone!"

"Exactly," Bonnie agreed. "We've just admitted to charging more than what the service we're providing is worth. If we balk and point to the terms of the contract, all the new decision-makers have to do is ask one question."

"And that is?"

"'Did our firm pay every invoice, in full and on time, during the first two years of the contract?' And Gambra did," Bonnie continued. "If they want to cancel the contract now, there's no reason for us to complain. We signed the deal. We agreed to the terms. If we don't know how to run our business to ensure we're adequately compensated for our efforts, why would that concern someone like the new CFO?"

"I guess it shouldn't," A.J. admitted, "but it sure feels funny saying so."

Why Good Clients
Fire
Great Companies

"When we agree to lower our fees in response to a competitive bid, the clients have to feel as if we've had our hand in their pockets," Bonnie continued. "When that happens, common sense tells you that any trust between us is gone. And we both know that no relationship can survive without trust."

"And if we don't come close to matching the bid, it's likely Gambra will take the lower bid and we're toast," A.J. replied.

"You said 'come close,'" Jack observed, jumping back into the discussion. "Why just 'come close?'"

"Well," A.J. replied, "any incumbent has an advantage."

"Oh?"

"Come on, Jack, you're the one who taught me that years ago. Clients don't want to change service management companies. It's a real hassle. They know it and we know it. So the incumbent usually can get away with charging a little bit more than the competitor. How much more depends on the situation and the relationships."

Why Good Clients
Fire
Great Companies

"Do you have an incumbent's advantage at Gambra?" Jack asked.

"Sure we do," came A.J.'s prompt reply.

"What's it worth?"

"I'd have to think about it before I could give you a number," A.J. replied. "But the tangible value is pretty much tied to three things: replacing our management team; buying or creating the operational and financial control systems to duplicate those we have in place; and coughing up the consulting fee they'd pay us to stay on board so their satisfaction scores and operational efficiency didn't slip while they made the changes.

"Of course," A.J. added as he thought out loud, "if they didn't want us to stay on in a consulting role, I guess you'd have to factor in something in lost efficiency for the learning curve they'd have to go through. But that would just be an estimate."

"One of the most powerful forces in any business is resistance to change," Jack affirmed. "True, it often works against us when we first assume responsibility for a client's operation and we're trying to implement our systems and processes. The one time it works *for* us is in retaining clients. We must use this natural resistance to change to our advantage with Gambra.

"Before Bonnie calls the CEO we'll need the numbers that define our incumbent's advantage—and they have to be real," Jack challenged, leaving no doubt as to the seriousness of his request.

"Okay," A.J. said, "I'll do my best."

"Bonnie," Jack said, shifting gears, "A.J.'s comments on the incumbent's advantage lead me into the last couple of points we need to discuss regarding Revelation X."

"And they are?"

"They have to do with the whole notion of 'making too much money' and how to protect long-term accounts from competitive threat," Jack answered.

"Do you think we're making too much at Gambra?" Bonnie asked somewhat defensively.

Why Good Clients
Fire
Great Companies

"Honestly, I have no idea. But I think I have a way for us to decide."

"How?" Bonnie's interest was piqued.

"Just a couple of questions," Jack began. "There are three components to understanding how much a piece of business is worth; that is, what the client should pay for the services provided. The first is the price a competent and financially disciplined competitor would bid to manage the services if the client put out a request for proposal today."

"How do we get that number?" Bonnie asked.

"We can't, directly," Jack responded. "But we can get very, very close."

"How?" she asked again.

"By getting your sales force involved," Jack said without hesitation. "Think about it," he continued. "They know Gambra's operation. They've helped you price the additional services you've sold over the years, and they've used Gambra often as a reference site. I'm sure they have a good sense of the numbers and the operation."

"And they know the competition," Bonnie said out loud, buying into Jack's suggestion. "I'll call our regional sales manager and ask her what she would bid if *we* were the competition and she wanted to take Gambra away from the incumbent."

"Given our time constraints, you may have to settle for a range of prices," Jack observed, "but it's the best estimate you'll have."

Bonnie immediately picked up the phone and called Alyson, her regional sales manager. The conversation ended in less than three minutes with Bonnie apologizing for the short notice but insisting that Alyson provide the number within the hour.

"What else do we need to know?" Bonnie asked, feeling a little uneasy about the stress she'd just caused her sales executive.

"We need to put a value to something that I call the Innovation Quotient^{sm}," Jack replied.

"Jeez, more names for things you've thought up? Do you

Why Good Clients
Fire
Great Companies

ever sleep at night?" came from A.J.

"It's the only way I can keep track of these things," Jack said. "Besides, I might want to write a book someday and trademark all this stuff so I can become rich and famous."

"Okay, I'll bite," A.J. said. "What's an Innovation Quotient?"

"It's the value a company enjoys when it provides a truly unique approach or innovation," Jack explained. "To put it another way, it's the increment in fee you can charge, over and above that of your competitors, because you can provide something unique that makes a real difference to the client. In short, it provides a ton of value!"

"Like our ServSense system," A.J. suggested.

"Right on, A.J.!" Jack exclaimed. "That's exactly what I'm talking about. No one can duplicate that system. It's the result of over five years of R&D, hundreds of thousands of dollars in investment, and a lot of blood, sweat, and tears by some very talented people within this company. The ServSense system sets this company apart from the competition and allows you to make significant reductions in the costs of client operations. That's worth something as long as you have effectively communicated it to the client and it has Relevant Value to them. I just call it—"

"The Innovation Quotient," A.J. said, smiling.

"You have several systems like ServSense installed at Gambra, don't you?" Jack asked.

"Nothing as clearly superior to the competition. But we do have a couple of processes in place that are superior in several areas."

"Great," Jack replied. "Here's another challenge: tell us how Gambra would value those features if their company lost the ability to use them in their operations."

"I'll have to give it some thought," A.J. cautioned.

"I realize that," Jack said, "but that's not all there is to it."

"Oh?"

"The Innovation Quotient is a double-edged sword, A.J. We get to capitalize on the positive value of systems like ServSense. But as both of you know, the competition has invested in capabilities that we can't currently duplicate. When that's the case, they get the benefit of their investments in incremental fees, and it becomes a minus on our side of the ledger."

"So if I understand you correctly, Jack, you want me to identify all the systems and processes that are unique to our company in delivering Relevant Value to the client. Then you want me to identify how much incremental compensation we could ask for the unique systems we provide to Gambra."

"Right so far," Jack confirmed.

"Next, you want me to identify the systems and processes that deliver value to the client that are unique to our competition. Then you want me to calculate how much incremental compensation they would ask for as a result of their unique systems and processes."

"Right again," Jack replied.

"And the difference between the two is the Innovation Quotient. I got it!" A.J. said triumphantly, beginning to calculate the difference between Service Enterprises' innovations and those of their most likely competitor.

Why Good Clients
Fire
Great Companies

"It's important that our IQ always be positive, isn't it, Jack?"

"You bet," Jack answered with a smile, seeing that A.J. already had internalized the lesson. "My retirement security depends on it."

"I guess mine does, too," A.J. said thoughtfully.

"So what we have then," Bonnie suggested as she focused on the problem at hand, "is a way to understand what the business is worth from the client's point of view." She moved to the board drew a sketch, and jotted down the formula.

Why Good Clients
Fire
Great Companies

What a Contract is Worth

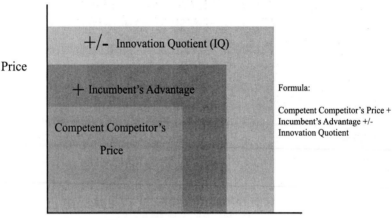

Price

+/- Innovation Quotient (IQ)

+ Incumbent's Advantage

Competent Competitor's

Price

Formula:

Competent Competitor's Price +
Incumbent's Advantage +/-
Innovation Quotient

Components

The contract is worth

- the price a competent and financially disciplined
  competitor is willing to bid to manage the operation as it
  exists today

- plus the incumbent's advantage (that is, the incremental
  fee the client would pay so the organization doesn't have
  to go through a change in management companies)

- and the Innovation Quotient (that is, the incremental fees we receive from the value of the true innovations we provide, minus the incremental fees our potential competitors would receive from the value of the innovations we can't currently duplicate)

"There," Bonnie reflected, "now I can visualize it as well."

"Bonnie," Jack cautioned as he admired her artwork, "that's a number we must have before you make your call to Gambra's CEO."

"Well, we have about three hours to develop it. I'll call Lindsey and ask her to get us some sandwiches and drinks."

As Bonnie moved toward the phone and A.J. started punching numbers into his calculator, Jack smiled to himself, sensing they had a real chance of keeping the business they'd worked so very hard to get.

Why Good Clients
Fire
Great Companies

It's Only
Worth What It's Worth

Why Good Clients *Fire* Great Companies

"I know, Alyson, I know," Bonnie said into the phone in a slightly exasperated tone. "I'm not asking you for that. I'm asking for your best estimate, that's all."

As she listened to Alyson's response, Bonnie could sense Jack and A.J.'s curiosity. "Thanks. In five minutes," she replied into the phone.

With that Bonnie hung up, sighed, and looked at Jack, saying, "She's reluctant to give me a number she can't absolutely guarantee."

"I'd imagine that's part of why you have one of the most effective sales organizations in the industry," Jack replied.

Bonnie smiled. They'd been working at generating the numbers for over two hours and the call to Gambra's CEO was less than forty-five minutes away. She could feel the tension building in her neck and shoulders.

"A.J., did you make the changes we discussed?" Jack began.

"I did, and it looks like the incumbent's advantage is between $30,000–$50,000."

Why Good Clients
Fire
Great Companies

"Okay," Jack replied, noting the figure on the board. "How much is the Innovation Quotient worth to us?"

"This is really a guess," A.J. responded uncertainly.

"I know, A.J., but it's the best we have. Besides, you know Gambra's operation and our competitor's abilities better than anyone."

"All right, I figure our ServSense system is worth an incremental $40,000 to us. It saves Gambra Incorporated three times that each year. I can document those numbers. The rest of our process and systems are worth maybe $10,000–$20,000 combined in incremental fees versus the competition."

"And the competition's advantages?" Jack asked, looking for the offset to the numbers A.J. had just provided.

"There's only one: their ProQual process. I wish we could duplicate that software tomorrow."

"From what I've heard, they've done a nice job with that system."

"They have, indeed," A.J. confirmed.

"What do you figure it's worth in incremental fees each year at an account the size of Gambra Incorporated?" Jack asked.

"Probably in the $25,000 range," A.J. replied. "At least that's what it looks like from where I sit. But Jack I really don't—"

"I know, A.J., we're looking for your judgment at this point, and that's all."

A.J. nodded, letting his frustration subside.

"That makes the net advantage to us about $70,000," Jack said, mentally subtracting the competitor's advantage of $25,000 from the total A.J. had supplied.

"Jack, I get the math, but I'd feel more comfortable if we used $50,000 instead. I just feel like some of the numbers I've given you are really soft," A.J. said in a final attempt to ease his anxiety.

"I've never gone wrong trusting your judgment. Fifty thousand it is," Jack replied.

Why Good Clients
Fire
Great Companies

Just as A.J. and Jack concluded their discussion of the incumbent's advantage and their IQ, the phone rang. It was Alyson with the final number they needed—the net dollar amount the competition would need to bid to take the Gambra Incorporated account as it existed today.

Okay, Alyson," Bonnie began. "Let me have it. . . Can't be!" she exclaimed, writing a figure on her legal pad. "How is that possible?"

Jack and A.J. exchanged curious glances as they tried to imagine the other side of the conversation.

"Explain that to me." Clearly, Bonnie was becoming a little irritated.

Jack knew Bonnie wouldn't increase Alyson's discomfort by putting her on speakerphone. He and A.J. could only listen intently as the monologue continued.

"You're sure?" Bonnie asked. ". . . I know, but as sure as you can be given the time constraints? So that's your range? That's what you'd suggest we bid if we were the competition? You know what's at stake here, don't you?"

Why Good Clients
Fire
Great Companies

After a minute or so, Bonnie said soothingly, "Listen, Alyson, I appreciate what you and your team have done on such short notice. Frankly, I'm just a little amazed and more than a little concerned about the number. It never occurred to me that the competition could do what we're doing for so much less. . . Okay. . . I understand your logic. . . Yes. . . I understand your math. . . Yes. . . Yes. . . We will. . . Thank you. You know how much I appreciate this. . . It's what I needed to know, even if it wasn't what I wanted to hear. Thanks again. I'll see you Friday."

With that, Bonnie hung up the phone and regarded Jack and A.J. with a look that was hard to describe. Confusion, fear, and anxiety played over her face, but balancing them was a calmness that Jack never would have expected.

"So, what's the good news?" he said, trying to relieve the tension.

"Alyson's team believes that if Gambra's business went out on an RFP today, the business could be won with a bid between $370,000 and $400,000 *in profit.*"

"No way!" A.J. erupted. "That's about a $100,000 less than our bottom line."

Why Good Clients
Fire
Great Companies

Jack wrote the figures on the board as A.J. and Bonnie stared at one another in disbelief.

"Obviously, you both have trouble swallowing that number," Jack offered.

"Jack, there's no way—" A.J. began only to be interrupted by Bonnie.

"A.J.," Bonnie said in a soothing voice, "let me give you the logic Alyson's team used."

For the next ten minutes, Bonnie explained the sales team's reasoning, which was nearly impeccable. Thanks to his intimate understanding of the operation, A.J. was able to shoot a couple of small holes in their math; but the net result was a number $75,000 less than what Service Enterprises was now charging Gambra Incorporated.

"If I understand this correctly," Jack said, walking to the board, "here's what the business is worth."

Jack entered the numbers behind Bonnie's earlier notes.

Why Good Clients
Fire
Great Companies

- The price a competent competitor is willing to bid to manage the operation as it exists today is $370,000.

- Our incumbent's advantage (that is, the incremental fee the client would pay to avoid a change in management companies) is $25,000.

- The Innovation Quotient (that is, the value of the true innovations we provide minus the value of the competition's innovations that we can't currently duplicate) is another $25,000.

"The business is worth $420,000," Jack said, adding up the numbers. "And how much are you earning from Gambra Incorporated?"

"We're projected to make $508,000," A.J. said without hesitation. He knew the numbers as well as he knew his way home.

"The difference is $88,000 and represents a 17.3 percent reduction in current costs—just about where the new CFO felt the numbers should be," Jack said matter-of-factly.

"But, Jack," A.J. protested, "if we reduce our costs by that

Why Good Clients
Fire
Great Companies

much now, we'll never regain the profits that were built into the proposal. You know that it costs us a ton of money to start these operations and that we 'make up' ground and profits later in the contract. That hasn't changed with their new acquisitions. We'll be in the red for at least a year on those start-ups."

"Deal structure certainly is a consideration here," Jack agreed, "but it's not going to be the determining factor in whether or not you keep Gambra."

Since time was short, he went directly to the heart of the matter: "I must say I don't understand why Service Enterprises allows a client to cancel a contract after we've made significant up-front investments. The only thing I can figure is that the cancellation clause is a holdover from the fee-for-service contracts. Allowing a thirty- or ninety-day cancellation clause to be incorporated into the terms made sense in those situations. The company had nothing at stake. We were paid for the services provided. If the client wanted to cancel with short notice, so be it. But since we've gone to these 'performance-based' contracts, where we invest a lot up front and get our pay-outs later, as the client's operations improve because of our efforts, there's no way I'd allow a client to walk away for any reason other than substandard performance."

Why Good Clients
Fire
Great Companies

Jack paused for breath, then continued: "And if it's industry practice to allow it, I'll just say that you're all asleep at the switch. It's got to change and it's going to take leadership to do it. But we're not going to settle the deal structure issues facing this industry now, so let's get focused on Gambra Incorporated, okay?"

A.J. spoke up: "What do you suggest we do? Should we give back the $88,000? We'd look awfully foolish if we did that now," he said, recalling his recent discussions of compensation with Gambra's new CFO.

"I'm going to suggest you give it back but not give them the money," Jack responded.

"I've got to hear this," Bonnie chuckled.

"Bet you have a name for this one, too," A.J. observed.

"I call it an *investment*, A.J., but if you think of a catchier name, let me know," Jack quipped. "Before we get into this," he continued, "I'll need to ask a couple of quick questions regarding Gambra."

Why Good Clients
Fire
Great Companies

Bonnie and A.J. nodded their agreement.

"Does Gambra have all the investment capital it needs?" Jack asked.

"Not by a long shot," came Bonnie's reply.

Picking up on Bonnie's assertion, A.J. marshaled his thoughts. He knew the information he was about to share was accurate. It came from one of Service Enterprises' corporate officers who, because the Web of Influence was practiced at all levels within Service Enterprises, had excellent relationships at Gambra's senior-management level.

As he spoke, A.J. knew he could also refer Jack to the T.A.R.P. folder, which contained notations of Gambra's cash-flow problems.

"Gambra is having performance issues at a number of its other subsidiaries," A.J. said. "They've milked their operations for years, and they've put off making the necessary investments. Those tactics allowed them to report good margins for a couple of years, but the problems have caught up with them."

Why Good Clients
Fire
Great Companies

"Frankly," Bonnie added, "I'm convinced that what's happened is a huge part of the reason for the change in their management."

"And does Gambra need to make capital investments in the operations we manage?" Jack asked.

"As far as I know," A.J. replied, "their capital budget for those operations is just a little over a quarter of a million dollars this year, mostly for new equipment that's well beyond when it should have been replaced."

"Great! That's all I need to know for right now," Jack said with a smile that seemed out of place given the discussion at hand. "Here's what I suggest," he said, moving toward the board.

Pointing to the 'Fees' line on the Revelation X illustration, Jack said, "Let me recap our conversation regarding the compensation. We agree that you can make too much money at an account. Right?"

A.J. and Bonnie nodded.

"We also agree that a client will pay only what a service is worth," Jack continued, "and what a service is worth is defined as:

- the price a competent and financially disciplined competitor is willing to bid to manage the operation as it exists today

- plus the incumbent's advantage (that is, the incremental fee the client would pay to avoid a change in management companies)

- and the Innovation Quotient (that is, the value of the true innovations we provide, minus the value of the competition's innovations that we can't currently duplicate)

Again, A.J. and Bonnie nodded their agreement.

"So any amount of money you're making over and above 'what the business is worth' *is not your money,*" Jack said emphatically.

Revelation X

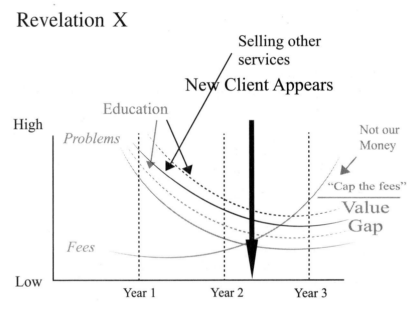

Reading the need for explanation on Bonnie and A.J.'s faces, he continued. "You're going to give that money back. The only choice you have is whether you'll give it back *proactively* or *reactively*. If you wait for a competitor to bid on the operation, you'll give the money back in a reactive way. And in the process, you're likely to undermine the trust that's supported the relationship. But if you give the money back proactively, you have many more choices. I suggest you give the money back without giving them the money. Here's how." Jack wrote on the board as he spoke:

Why Good Clients
Fire
Great Companies

Use the money over and above what the business is worth to invest in two areas that will give Service Enterprises an ongoing advantage:

• Erecting obstacles to competitive entry

• Strengthening barriers to client exit

He explained: "Gambra needs equipment in the operations we manage, but they're short of cash. Put on your win-win hat. Let's make the investments for them, allowing them to use the cash they would have invested in those operations in other parts of their company."

"But how does that help us?" A.J. asked.

"Simple, A.J., we 'own' the equipment in which we're investing until it's fully depreciated. Then we turn it over to Gambra. We amortize our investment by charging depreciation to the cost of operation each year so that we can recover our capital."

"I get it, Jack!" A.J. said, his eyes widening with excitement. "As long as we own the equipment, if any competitor tries to underbid us, we just take the equipment with us when the contract terminates. Gambra, or more likely the new management services company, would have to replace the equipment."

"Actually, A.J., it would work a little differently in practice," Jack explained, "but you're absolutely right about the impact. If Gambra canceled the contract, Gambra would owe us the undepreciated value of the equipment. While that might not prevent them from making a change in the first year or two, it would have a significant impact on their decisions after we made several years' worth of investments. These investments would become barriers to our competitors in that they couldn't enter into an agreement if they had to come up with a significant amount of cash to 'buy us out.'"

"And this strategy puts up barriers to exit for Gambra Incorporated," A.J. said, grasping the essence of Jack's suggestion, "because, if they decided to run the operations again on their own, they'd have to come up with a lot of cash at the transition point. And the investments are made only with the increment that's over and above 'what the business is worth' each year," he added enthusiastically, "so we're using money that we would eventually give back anyway in a reactive situation. And if we're smart, we can get a lot of mileage out of those investments and strengthen the relationship to boot."

"And it doesn't necessarily need to be equipment," Jack explained. "It could be an investment in an on-site trainer or a local recruiting effort if that's what was required to make a difference, but they couldn't afford to do it themselves."

"Not a bad approach—in theory," Bonnie admonished.

"Not a bad approach in practice, either," Jack countered. "Let's get to work on how you might position what we've discussed earlier with Gambra's new CEO. Here's what we know . . ."

For the next twenty minutes, Jack, Bonnie, and A.J. feverishly reviewed the results of the processes Jack had introduced that morning. Each process helped them discover something they could use to prevent the cancellation from becoming "official."

They answered the four key questions Jack had asked:

1. Gambra hired us because. . .

2. Gambra will renew our contract only if. . .

3. If Gambra cancels our contract, the major thing they lose
   is. . .

4. The *one thing* we need to do to retain Gambra's business
   is. . .

These answers coupled with the work they had done on
creating Relevant Value gave them ideas Bonnie knew would
intrigue Gambra's CEO. But what allowed her to mentally
shift gears was the realization that a service is worth only
what it's worth. No more, no less. Through Revelation X, she
grasped this fundamental truth: the only thing that matters is
the Relevant Value being provided *now*.

Bonnie also understood that she could use the money Service
Enterprises was making over and above what was "fair" to
protect the account. She could proactively invest in barriers
to competitive entry and client exit, or she could wait until
the day a competitor bid and she was forced to lower her
fees. Her choice was simple.

It also occurred to Bonnie that she could use the same
process to *increase* Service Enterprises' compensation at
other accounts where the formula showed them to be making
less than what was fair to make. But that analysis would wait
for another day.

Why Good Clients.
Fire
Great Companies

As the three colleagues talked about the phone call and the strategy needed to buy them some time, Bonnie gave Jack a wink and smiled. Because of his concern and guidance, she felt they had an honest chance of retaining Gambra Incorporated.

The Good News

Why Good Clients
Fire
Great Companies

Jack received the package early Saturday morning. It was something he'd looked forward to since Bonnie had given him the good news regarding Gambra's decision to remain under agreement with his old firm.

Bonnie's call to Gambra's CEO that day had opened the door to further discussion. Service Enterprises' Web of Influence had served them well as A.J. and his team sought coaching in preparation for their review with the new CEO's team and board.

What became clear was that the CFO didn't want to change management companies but felt Gambra Incorporated had little choice if the firm was to reduce short-term operating costs. And she was very clear that Gambra's survival depended on turning things around quickly.

Jack heard through his grapevine that Bonnie and A.J. absolutely wowed 'em at the Gambra Incorporated board meeting earlier in the month. In fact, his sources confirmed that several board members had privately wished all their outsourcing partners would demonstrate similar win-win attitudes.

Why Good Clients
Fire
Great Companies

As much as retaining Gambra Incorporated pleased Jack, he was most impressed that Bonnie had taken it upon herself to change the industry's practice regarding unilateral cancellation clauses in performance-based contracts. If anyone could lead the industry to the path of reason, she could.

He knew that ultimately, more reasonable cancellation criteria would find its way into Service Enterprises' Right Clients/Right Terms criteria and that the concepts of Relevant Value and the lessons of Revelation X would be intertwined with the other processes of the Clients for Life client-retention process.

Jack even allowed himself to get a bit emotional about Bonnie's attitude, which spurred her to fight to retain every client, confident of her company's ability to deliver Relevant Value. Service Enterprises had always been so much more than a job to him, and he knew she felt the same.

Tearing open the FedEx package, Jack found a thank-you note and a neatly framed four-color rendering of Revelation X. As always, Bonnie's thanks came from the heart. And as always, Jack felt proud to be associated with her and young managers like A.J., who would soon inherit more authority and responsibility within the company.

Why Good Clients
Fire
Great Companies

But everyone else in the house was waiting for the main contents of the package itself—Jack's compensation for the consulting he'd provided.

As his granddaughters, Kimmy, Missy, and Lauren, and his grandson, Casey, gathered around, Jack tore off the wrapping paper. There it was, his customary retainer: a box of chocolate-covered cherries.

Now they had everything they needed to enjoy the morning's cartoons.

Appendix:

What Your Clients Won't Tell You and Your Managers Don't Know

Why Good Clients
Fire
Great Companies

Appendix

I. The Clients for Life Philosophy

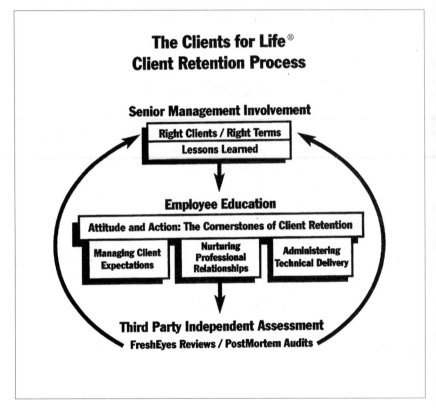

**The Clients for Life®
Client Retention Process**

Senior Management Involvement

Right Clients / Right Terms

Lessons Learned

Employee Education

Attitude and Action: The Cornerstones of Client Retention

Managing Client Expectations

Nurturing Professional Relationships

Administering Technical Delivery

Third Party Independent Assessment
FreshEyes Reviews / PostMortem Audits

Why Good Clients
Fire
Great Companies

A. Client retention is not a "program," it's an ongoing commitment to your clients and colleagues.

II. The Cornerstones of Client Retention

A. Attitude and Action are the cornerstones of the Clients for Life philosophy.

1. Attitude: We never lose a client that meets our criteria. We're proactive in helping the client solve problems and take advantage of opportunities.

2. Action: When and if we perceive a threat, we take whatever action is necessary to protect the account.

Why Good Clients
Fire
Great Companies

B. Encouraging employees to assimilate this philosophy takes time—they must experience your commitment to become believers themselves.

C. All clients should be crucial to you or you shouldn't be doing business with them.

III. Right Clients/Right Terms℠

A. The senior executive, and his or her staff, is responsible for developing and later articulating the criteria that describe the "right clients" and detail the "right terms."

B. All senior managers should be involved in the following process:

Why Good Clients
Fire
Great Companies

Step 1: Ask the senior managers in attendance to think about and capture the "demographic and psychographic profile" of the "ideal" client.

Step 2: Ask the senior managers in attendance to share their descriptions one criteria at a time, going from person to person, until all the criteria are captured on flip charts and the sheets have been tacked up on the walls of the meeting room.

Step 3: Facilitate a discussion of the criteria. Look for early consensus. Explore conflicting experiences. Encourage debate among the attendees.

Step 4: Identify the "must have" criteria regarding the "right clients" that will not be violated—no matter how good the terms.

Step 5: Conduct the same process regarding the "right terms."

Note: The results should range from "10 to 12" demographic and psychographic criteria. These terms must be clearly articulated by the senior executive and interpreted consistently within the organization.

> C. The Right Clients/Right Terms criteria should be reviewed every six months.

> > 1. A change in key decision-makers is the most common reason to review an account.

> D. When a client is no longer willing to do business under the "right terms," resigning an account is a proactive management decision.

Why Good Clients
Fire
Great Companies

1. It's more profitable to resign an account that no longer fits your criteria than to continue to do business at unacceptable profit levels.

E. How you close a contract is just as important as how you open one.

2. As soon as you decide to resign an account, devise an exit plan which doesn't divulge proprietary information but keeps the client's operation running.

2. An "official" closing takes place when the firms cease to do business under contract, but unofficial relationships can last a lifetime.

3. Stay in touch—keeping the personal contacts does take effort, but not as much

Why Good Clients
   Fire
Great Companies

effort as selling a new client from scratch.

4. Former clients can provide a constant source of leads and referrals.

IV. **Keeping What You've Worked So Hard to Get**

A. Client retention isn't an event. It's a daily process.

B. The worst possible time to renew a contract is when it's due for renewal. If you wait until then, you lose the incumbent's advantage.

C. Provided you've taken the right clients under the right terms, your responsibility is to protect the client's interests—which are the same as yours.

1. Protecting the client's interests dramatically reduces the likelihood of

2. When a confrontation does occur, its' focus
is on the client's business, not on
your firm's profits.

3. You must care enough to confront the client
on issues of concern.

V. **Sharing the Lessons Learned**sm

A. The Lessons Learned are the handful of reasons
that explain the majority of the losses historically
incurred.

1. Senior managers are responsible
for identifying the Lessons Learned,
communicating these lessons to their
employees and sharing the tactics
they've used to eliminate these threats.

Why Good Clients
Fire
Great Companies

      2. Everyone is responsible for taking the action indicated by the senior managers when one of the threats presents itself.

    B. When people change, everything has the potential to change.

      1. A new client decision-maker might see things so differently as to no longer be the right client under the right terms.

VI. **Start-Up: A Crucial Time**

    A. All managers should go through a sales and negotiating course to improve their skills when interacting with clients and with their own managers who influence the start-up process.

B. Always start up according to the client's expectations.

C. The Transition Meeting is a process that must take place before a new contract can begin operations.

D. Delay your own firm's SOP (Standard Operating Practices) if it creates a conflict with the client's expectations regarding the start-up.

> 1. Delaying your SOP does not mean deceiving your own firm; it simply means using your talents to sell management on the need to be patient in implementing some of the required procedures.

VII. **The Transition Meeting**sm

A. This meeting's attendees include everyone in the client's decision-making unit and the service provider's sales rep, the operations manager responsible for implementing the contract, and the business unit manager ultimately responsible for the company's performance.

B. The Transition Meeting also includes any new client decision-makers who have assumed responsibility since the signing of the contract.

C. All client and service provider participants write down their immediate, short-term, and long-term expectations.

D. These written statements become the basis for open discussion between firms.

E. In the unlikely event that the clients are unwilling to abide by the "right terms"—after exhausting all possible ways of finding a "win-win" solution—the discussion should shift to the creation of an exit plan.

* Unless you are willing to walk away, you cannot negotiate effectively.

VIII. Sales and Operations: A Consistent Message and Mission

> A. Expect your clients to have expectations you didn't expect they would have—as long as those expectations don't violate the "right clients/right terms" criteria, that's OK.

> B. Sales reps can't be expected to foresee all client expectations, but they must be responsible team members.

> C. The Transition Meeting is the vehicle that keeps sales people from promising more than operations can deliver.

Why Good Clients
Fire
Great Companies

1. Representatives from sales and operations must attend the transition Meeting.

2. At the meeting, operations managers can refuse to accept the assignment.

3. No contract is valid until after the Transition Meeting, which is the final stage of negotiations.

4. The contract's language must include the expectations of both companies and must specify that the Transition Meeting will make all negotiations final.

5. Operations must not begin work without a signed contract.

6. No commissions should be paid to the sales staff until after a successful Transition Meeting.

D. The notion that growth comes from your next client is a fallacy.

    1. In an existing business of any size, to deliver the profit of one existing client takes at least three new clients of the same size.

    2. Success depends not upon growth but upon **profitable** growth.

IX. **If You Leave Client Retention to Chance…**

A. If you leave client retention to chance, chances are you're going to lose clients. Client retention demands a formal process.

B. To avoid 30% of lost clients, educate your employees in three key areas:

Why Good Clients
Fire
Great Companies

1. Managing client expectations.

> 2. Developing relationships at all levels of both organizations.

> 3. Delivering the technical aspects of your service in a way that's consistent with the client's expectations.

C. To avoid 20% of lost clients, use an independent 3rd party to help assess the status of your clients and contracts.

> 1. Customer satisfaction surveys don't work in a management services environment.

> 2. FreshEyes Reviews monitor current client satisfaction.

3. PostMortem Audits reveal reasons for client defections and help management avoid repeating mistakes.

X. Managing Client Expectations

A. The next thirty percent of potential losses can be saved by educating your managers. The first piece of information they need is how to understand and manage their clients' expectations.

B. Expectations are formed from prior personal experiences and all forms of communication— particularly those used during the selling process.

1. To judge our performance, clients use their expectations of what will happen and not what "really" happens.

Why Good Clients
Fire
Great Companies

2. Client expectations are constantly changing as clients have new experiences and are exposed to new communications.

3. By using the power of personal communications, it's possible to create, influence and manage client expectations, but not to control them.

4. The secret to understanding client expectations is to ASK.

   a. Ask your clients about their expectations on a quarterly basis to stay in touch with client needs, reinforce your value to the client and obtain funding or approvals for future projects.

C. When dealing with clients, deliver superior performance, but beware of the Expectations Paradox.[sm]

Why Good Clients
Fire
Great Companies

1. Clients for Life defines superior
performance as performance that exceeds
the client's expectations.

2. Exceed the expectation, but by just a little
or suffer the consequences of the
Expectations Paradox.

3. The Expectations Paradox strikes when
you provide the client with experiences that
you can not deliver consistently.

4. Clients will accept the service provider's
limits under three conditions:

      a. The client trusts you.

Why Good Clients
Fire
Great Companies

b. The limits are real.

c. The competition can't do better.

XI. **Nurturing Professional Relationships**

A. Like personal relationships, professional relationships flourish when they're based on trust and respect.

1. Trust is created by consistently demonstrating candor, competency, and concern.

2. Trust takes a long time to build but a split second to lose.

3. Respect is gained when you take a stand on the things people know are right.

B. Always weave and maintain a Web of Influence[sm].

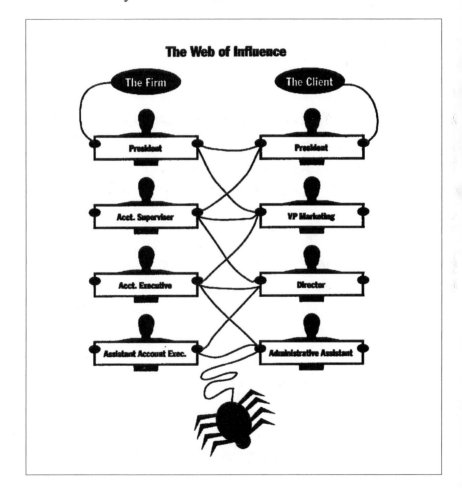

Why Good Clients
Fire
Great Companies

1. Never let the contract depend on one business* relationship, no matter how high in the client's organization.

* A business relationship means that your client knows you, trusts and respects you and will meet with you—provided you have a valid business reason for meeting.

2. Every one of our managers must be tied to three in the client's organization.

3. The Web of Influence must include the clients that can hire us, fire us or significantly influence that decision.

C. Create a database of information on each client.

1. This information should include the client's home town, college attended, hobbies, favorite restaurants, clubs and associations, etc.

2. A database like this is crucial to maintaining client relationships as people transfer within the company or leave to pursue their own careers.

XII. Solving Problems and Delivering Innovation

A. From a technical standpoint, clients expect a services provider to solve their problems and bring innovation to their business.

1. The key to solving a client's problems is agreement on what the problems are and understanding the priorities the client assigns to getting them fixed.

2. Innovation is something clients are not yet doing for themselves.

Why Good Clients
Fire
Great Companies

> 3. Innovation need not be a newly acquired skill to be a revelation to the client.

B. Document your successes; your failures will document themselves.

> 1. Documentation of success will leave a paper trail beneficial to your organization in times of change.

XIII. The FreshEyes℠ Review and the PostMortemAudit℠

A. Both of these processes must be done by unbiased, third-party individuals or organizations or the information may not only be suspect but truly counterproductive. Advanced and highly developed probing, listening and writing skills are required to elicit, verify and communicate what is learned.

Why Good Clients
Fire
Great Companies

Action must be taken based on the information each of the processes provides.

B. The FreshEyes Review should be conducted annually at all key accounts and/or when a significant event or change occurs for a client.

    1. The FreshEyes Review asks these questions:

        a. How are we living up to the client's expectations?

        b. How good are the relationships between the people representing the organizations?

        c. How effective is the delivery of our technical services?

C. A PostMortem Audit should be conducted within two months of the time the contract is canceled.

1. PostMortem Audits ask these questions:

a. Where did we fail to live up to the client's expectations?

b. Where did our Web of Influence break down?

c. Where did the technical aspects of our service fall short?

D. Mistakes can be corrected only after they've been acknowledged.

E. To reinforce your value to a client, engage in the Transition Lite exercise. Review with the client the condition of the business when you first assumed responsibility for the account, its condition now, and the client's expectations for the future.

Why Good Clients
Fire
Great Companies

Afterword

John Gamble is the founder of Tenacity Incorporated and leads the firm's development efforts in finding and teaching more effective, productive and profitable ways to build client equity through managing client retention for the long term.

Steve Wurzbacher is a Tenacity Principal and the firm's longest tenure partner. He manages brand development and social media functions for the firm.

Tenacity Incorporated and the Clients for Life[sm] client retention process are currently protecting over $20 billion in service management contracts.

Tenacity Incorporated is headquartered in Atlanta, Georgia and is available to work with service management firms of all sizes in tailoring, implementing and imprinting into their culture, the practical aspects of the Clients for Life process. John and Steve are also available for speaking engagements.

Please contact us at www.tenacity.com or write us at 550 Oakhaven Drive, Suite 2-B, Roswell, Georgia 30075 or call at 770-642-0701.

Why Good Clients
Fire
Great Companies